GIANT
KINDERGARTEN

This workbook belongs to

....

Dear Parents,

Welcome to the *Giant Kindergarten* workbook!

The fun activities in this workbook will reinforce key learning concepts to help prepare your child for first grade. They will help build your child's pen-control skills and increase his or her knowledge of the ABCs and 123s. Here are some tips to ensure your child gets the most from this book.

- Look at the pages with your child, ensuring he or she knows what to do before starting.

- Make the activity sessions positive experiences. Praise your child's efforts, and point out when progress has been made through practice.

- Discourage your child from rushing. You can help him or her focus on the current page by removing it using the perforations.

- Plan for your child to do only one or two pages a day, and encourage him or her to look forward to completing another activity on a different day.

- If your child makes a mistake, help foster a mindset that views mistakes as learning opportunities and suggest that your child try again.

- If possible, complete the activities within each section in order because some activities build on one another.

- Relate the learning to things in your child's world. For example, if your child is working on a page about the letter *b*, play a fun game finding things around your home that begin with *b*, such as a *bed* and a *book*.

- There are stickers to use at the back of the book. You can use them as reward stickers, or your child can use them to decorate the pages in any way she or he likes.

We wish your child hours of enjoyment while building a strong start at school!

Scholastic Early Learning

Contents

The Letter A

Circle the things that start with **a**.

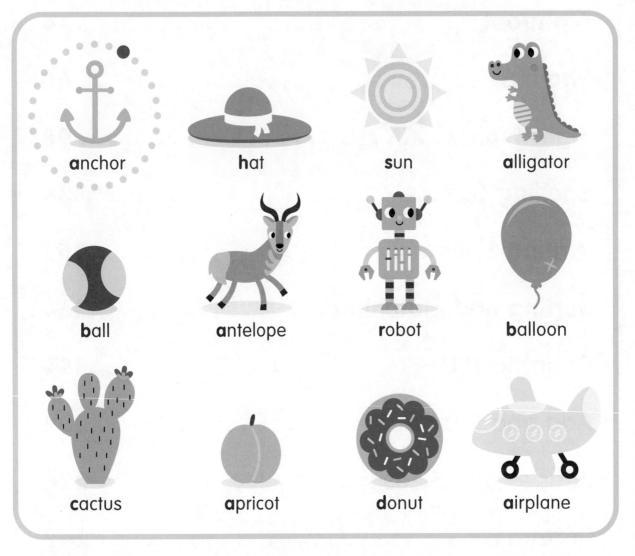

anchor | hat | sun | alligator

ball | antelope | robot | balloon

cactus | apricot | donut | airplane

Trace and write uppercase and lowercase **a**'s.

Ant's Adventure

Draw a line linking the things that start with **a** to help the **a**nt reach the **a**pple.

start → **a**nt	**a**stronaut	**s**kirt	**o**ctopus	**h**ouse
cheese	**a**xe	**m**edal	**f**ridge	**b**us
penguin	**a**rrow	**a**crobat	**l**emon	**j**ewel
fairy	**l**obster	**a**bacus	**t**elescope	**w**hale
canoe	**k**ite	**a**lpaca	**a**mbulance	→ finish **a**pple

The Letter B

Write the missing **b**'s in these words.

b̲ arn   cra__

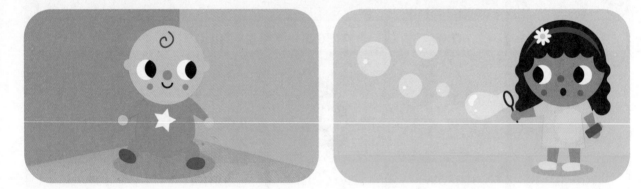

__a__y   __u__ __les

Trace and write uppercase and lowercase **b**'s.

Bella's Boutique

Bella's **B**outique only sells things that start with **b**.
Circle the items **B**ella can sell at her **b**outique.
Put an X over the items **B**ella can't sell.

buttons   **s**carf   **b**oots

pajamas   Bella's Boutique   **d**ress

bows   **c**oat   **b**ooks   **b**ackpack

The Letter C

Trace the **c**'s with your finger. Then draw lines to match the words to the uppercase or lowercase letter.

carrot

caterpillar

Connor

Camilla

Canada

clothes

Trace and write uppercase and lowercase **c**'s.

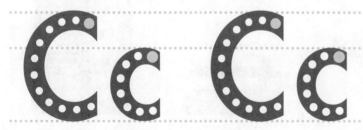

Cat Camouflage

Find and point to the **c**ute **c**at hiding among the **c**ows.
Then find and circle 5 **c**'s.

The Letter D

Find and circle the words that start with **d**.
They can go across or down.

a	y	m	g	k	t	h	w	v
l	n	d	a	d	d	y	k	b
d	e	c	p	s	g	t	o	d
s	g	p	z	b	h	p	v	a
r	h	n	s	l	y	e	d	n
d	e	s	s	e	r	t	r	c
r	u	o	j	i	k	n	f	e
u	k	q	o	t	l	u	s	w
m	d	c	m	p	d	i	u	j

drum

dessert

daddy

dance

Trace and write uppercase and lowercase **d**'s.

10

Duck Pond

Color the ducks with uppercase **D**'s yellow.
Color the ducks with lowercase **d**'s pink.

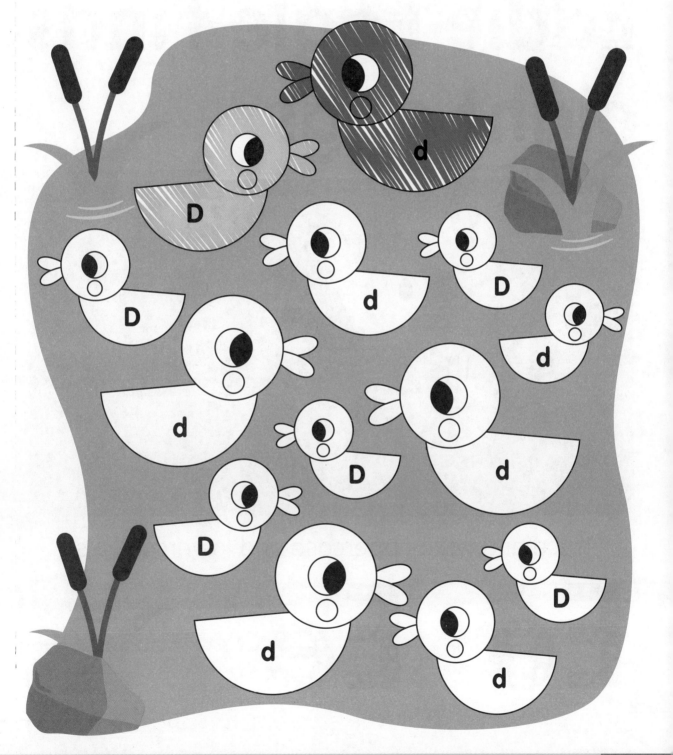

The Letter E

Trace the **e**'s. Then find and circle **e**ight **e**ggs.

Eddie Eagle finds eight eggs.

Trace and write uppercase and lowercase **e**'s.

E is for Earth

Use the color key to reveal the **E**arth.

Key: E = green, e = blue, D = orange, d = yellow

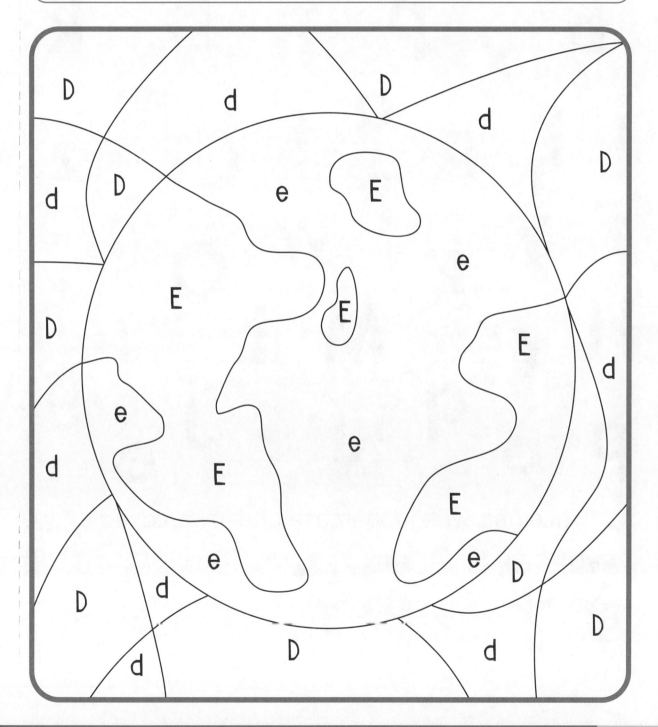

The Letter F

Find and circle 3 uppercase **F**'s.
Then find and underline 3 lowercase **f**'s.

b x p h D k
i l a f m z
F T C
f Y w O b
K M L s F
H f g
P o q N F J e

Trace and write uppercase and lowercase **f**'s.

F is for Farm

Search the **f**arm scene for these things that start with **f**. Check the boxes when you find them.

☐ 1 **f**ox   ☐ 2 **f**armers   ☐ 3 **f**ish   ☐ 4 **f**lowers

The Letter G

Circle the things that start with **g**.

horse

monster

van

gift

goose

sweater

flower

guitar

dinosaur

gate

clock

goat

Trace and write uppercase and lowercase **g**'s.

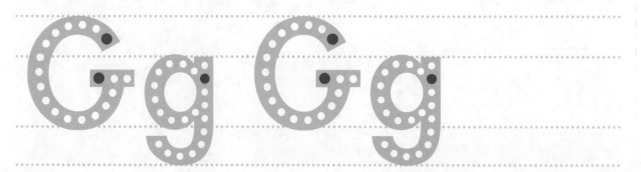

G is for Giraffe

Find and point to 5 **g**iraffes.
Then find and circle 5 **g**'s.

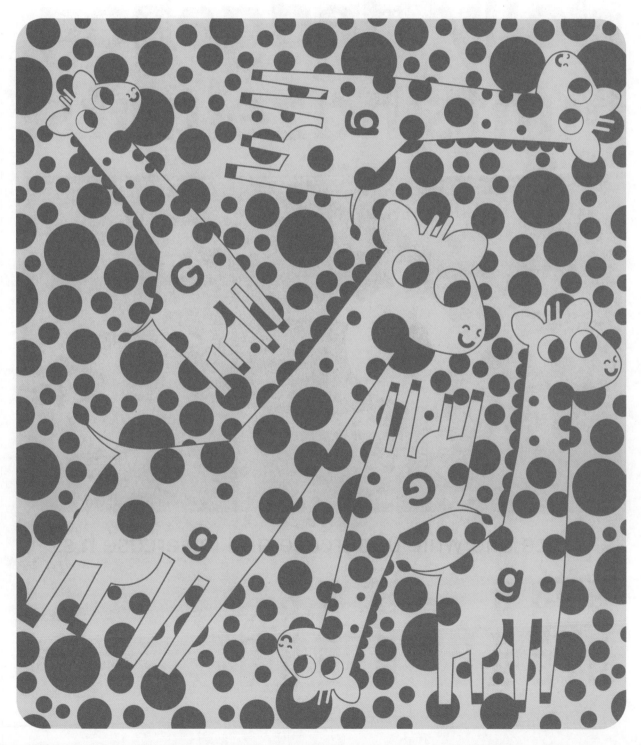

The Letter H

Trace the **h**'s. Then find and circle 7 **h**idden **h**azelnuts.

Holly Hedgehog hunts hazelnuts.

Trace and write uppercase and lowercase **h**'s.

Hungry Horse

Draw a line linking the things that start with **h** to **h**elp the **h**orse reach the **h**ay.

start →

horse	heart	house	hippo	T-shirt
pancakes	leaf	puzzle	helmet	sled
frog	socks	hen	hamburger	orange
violin	coral	helicopter	bug	car
digger	tree	hive	hammer	hay

→ finish

The Letter I

Write the missing **i**'s in these words.

__nk   __gloo

k__w__   __c__cles

Trace and write uppercase and lowercase **i**'s.

Iguana Island

Can you reach the uppercase **I** on **I**guana **I**sland?
Collect all the lowercase **i**'s along the way.

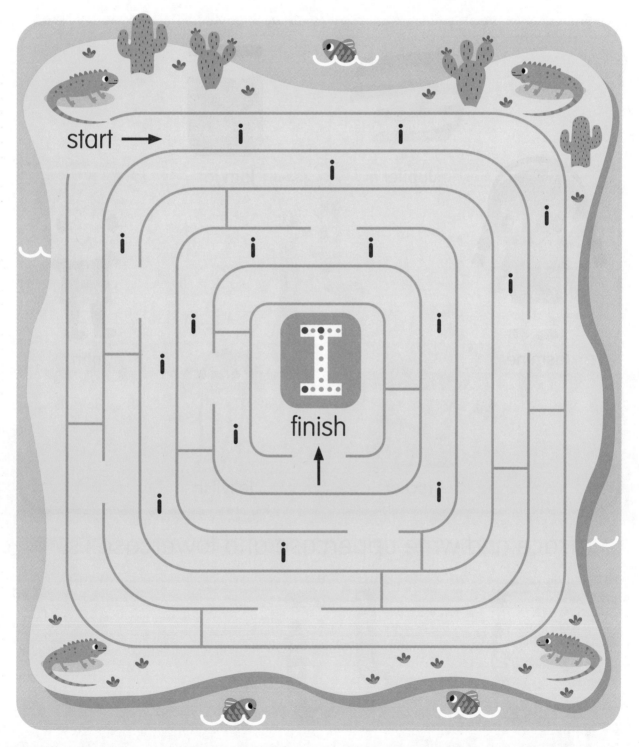

The Letter J

Trace the **j**'s with your finger. Then draw lines to match the words to the uppercase or lowercase letter.

Jupiter

jam jar

Jasmine

John

jacket

jellyfish

Trace and write uppercase and lowercase **j**'s.

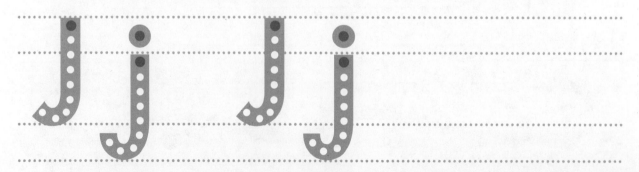

Juggling J's

Color the **j**uggling balls with uppercase **J**'s green.
Color the **j**uggling balls with lowercase **j**'s red.

The Letter K

Find and circle the words that start with **k**.
They can go across or down.

kettle

key

koala

kick

s	t	u	h	o	f	p	d	k
k	h	k	b	g	x	y	a	m
f	j	e	m	k	o	a	l	a
w	l	t	p	v	g	h	n	v
s	d	t	q	e	r	r	k	b
a	o	l	w	g	b	e	i	q
n	k	e	y	p	z	j	c	v
i	u	r	e	a	s	i	k	o
j	i	c	n	k	l	c	r	g

Trace and write uppercase and lowercase **k**'s.

K k K k

K is for Kayak

Search the **k**aya**k**ing scene for things that start with **k**.
Check the boxes when you find them.

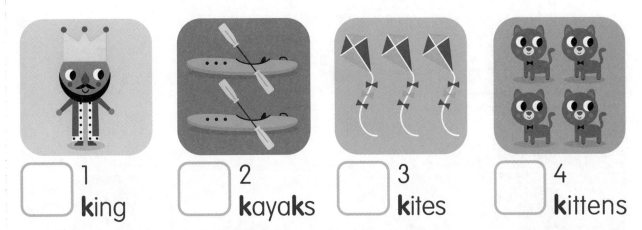

☐ 1 **k**ing
☐ 2 **k**aya**k**s
☐ 3 **k**ites
☐ 4 **k**ittens

The Letter L

Circle the things that start with **l**.

boat · trumpet · shoes · lemon

lollipop · baseball · leaf · mirror

shell · doll · ladybug · pizza

Trace and write uppercase and lowercase **l**'s.

Lurking Lion

Find and point to the lion lurking in the leopards' lair.
Then find and circle 5 l's.

The Letter M

Trace the **m**'s. Then find and circle 6 **m**elon slices.

Mimi Mouse munched melon.

Trace and write uppercase and lowercase **m**'s.

Mm Mm

Mark's Market

Mark's Market only sells things that start with **m**.
Circle the items **M**ark can sell at his **m**arket.
Put an X over the items **M**ark can't sell.

melon

marbles

pie

watch

MARK'S MARKET

$2

MILK

milk

mug

kite

mittens

The Letter N

Find and circle 3 uppercase **N**'s.
Then find and underline 3 lowercase **n**'s.

g N d E T I m
i
n S M N o e a
b V O R j T h x
Q R Z s g
r f t k n
N Y W n B K Y

Trace and write uppercase and lowercase **n**'s.

Nn Nn

Nightingale's Nest

Draw a line linking the things that start with **n** to help the **n**ightingale reach its **n**est.

start → **n**ightingale	**n**ecklace	**g**oose	**l**amp	**c**ap
xylophone	**n**ut	**c**rayon	**y**ogurt	**f**ire
sandwich	**n**arwhal	**m**otorcycle	**b**ee	**g**ate
shorts	**n**urse	**t**riangle	**c**astle	**s**hip
eel	**n**et	**n**oodles	**n**ewt	→ finish **n**est

The Letter O

Write the missing **o**'s in these words.

__tter   her__

__ct__pus   t __mat__

Trace and write uppercase and lowercase **o**'s.

Orange Maze

Can you reach the uppercase **O** inside the **o**range?
Collect all the lowercase **o**'s along the way.

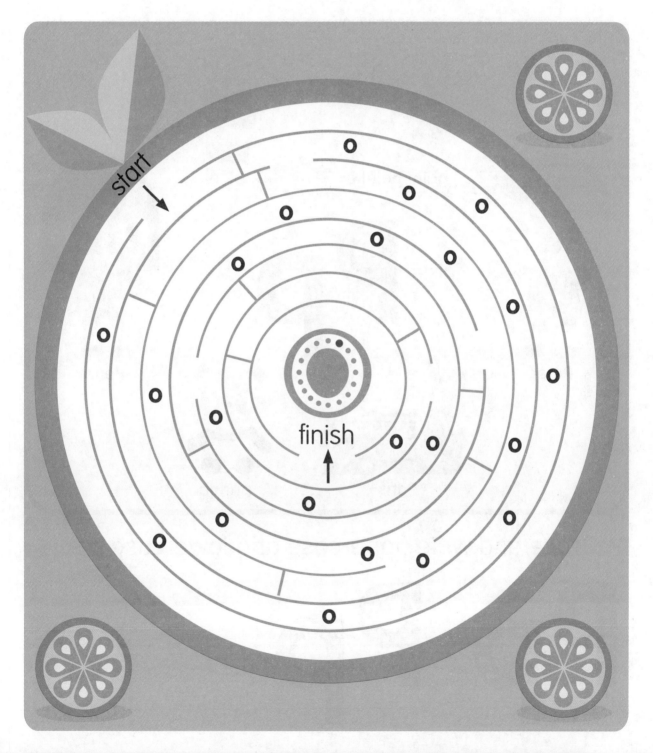

The Letter P

Trace the **p**'s with your finger. Then draw lines to match the words to the uppercase or lowercase letter.

paint palette

plant

Peter

Penny

Paris

panda

Trace and write uppercase and lowercase **p**'s.

Piper's Pot

Piper is making a stew using only foods that start with **p**.
Circle the foods **P**iper **p**uts in her **p**ot.
Put an X over the foods **P**iper doesn't **p**ut in her **p**ot.

pepper carrot **p**umpkin

onion **t**omato

peas **p**otatoes **b**roccoli

The Letter Q

Find and circle 3 uppercase **Q**'s.
Then find and underline 3 lowercase **q**'s.

d M q d O b w
t u I m r
p Q p l Q
S o E B T
V s B Z R q
b q z d g
i T O F Q g P

Trace and write uppercase and lowercase **q**'s.

Questioning Q's

Color the question marks with uppercase **Q**'s yellow.
Color the question marks with lowercase **q**'s pink.

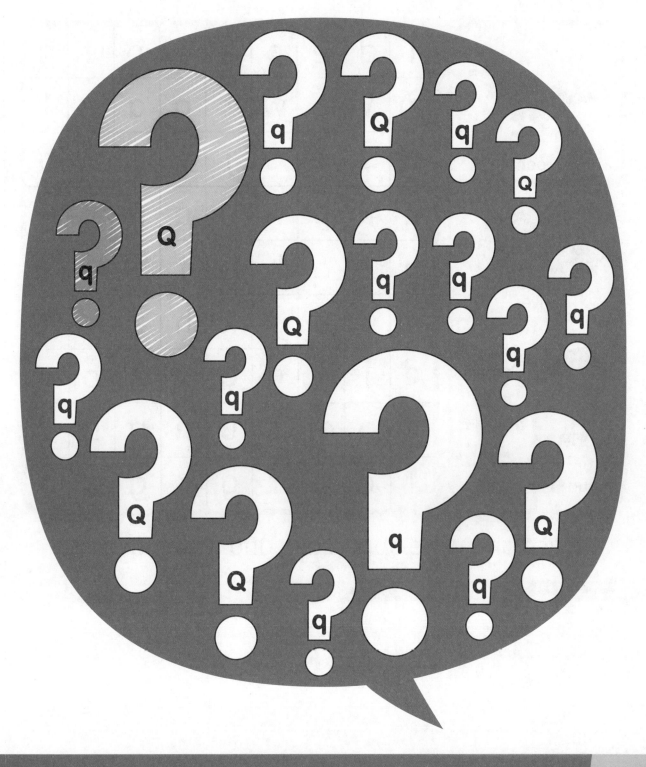

The Letter R

Find and circle the words that start with **r**.
They can go across or down.

l	d	e	p	s	i	o	t	n
m	y	e	w	r	o	a	r	l
n	s	r	c	j	v	e	i	h
d	k	p	h	a	q	n	v	y
h	r	o	b	o	t	f	e	z
t	r	u	f	k	h	z	r	l
d	j	i	a	q	u	b	o	u
e	o	m	r	u	n	p	n	v
l	c	a	f	g	k	g	x	b

roar

river

run

robot

Trace and write uppercase and lowercase **r**'s.

Rabbit Run

Draw a line linking the things that start with **r**
to help the **r**abbit **r**each the **r**adish.

start ➔ **r**abbit	**r**ing	**r**ainbow	**b**ear	**c**andle
seahorse	**i**sland	**r**ocket	**s**ofa	**j**et
moon	**t**ruck	**r**ice	**u**kulele	**d**ragon
squirrel	**f**lag	**r**ug	**r**ose	**p**izza
vase	**h**elmet	**b**agel	**r**adio	➔ finish **r**adish

39

The Letter S

Trace the **s**'s. Then find and circle 6 **s**ocks.

Susie searches for six socks.

Trace and write uppercase and lowercase **s**'s.

Striped Snakes

Find and point to 6 **s**nakes hiding in the **s**tripes.
Outline the **s**nake that makes an **s** **s**hape.

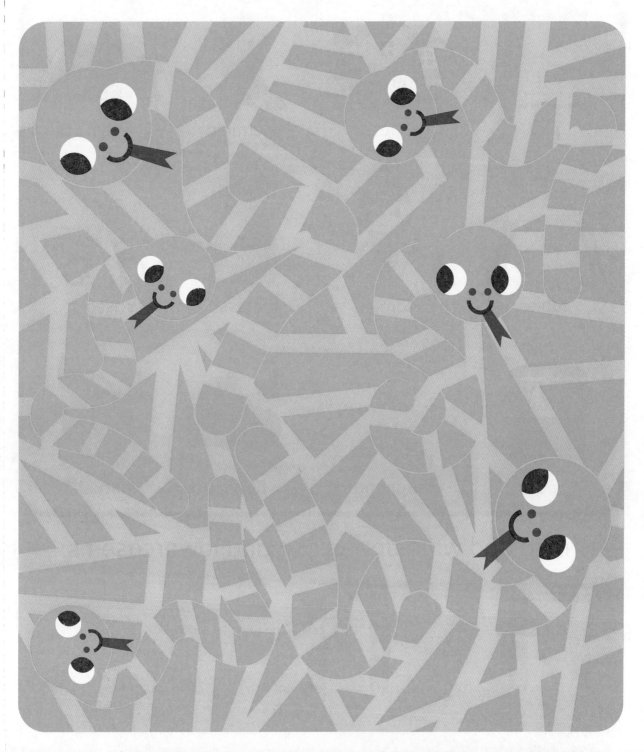

The Letter T

Circle the things that start with **t**.

pig   **h**ouse   **m**ermaid   **t**ent

table   **f**armer   **d**ress   **s**cissors

toy box   **b**anana   **t**urkey   **r**ocket

Trace and write uppercase and lowercase **t**'s.

Turtle Trick

Find and point to the **turtle** trying to be a **t**iger.
Then find and circle 5 **t**'s.

The Letter U

Find and circle 3 uppercase **U**'s.
Then find and underline 3 lowercase **u**'s.

W V U n Q B u O
F t w D a A n S
T L w E s U P M i
u l r b m V q w
I n u g Y n U

Trace and write uppercase and lowercase **u**'s.

Uu Uu

U is for Umbrella

Use the color key to reveal the **u**mbrella.

Key: U = orange, u = red, T = blue, t = purple

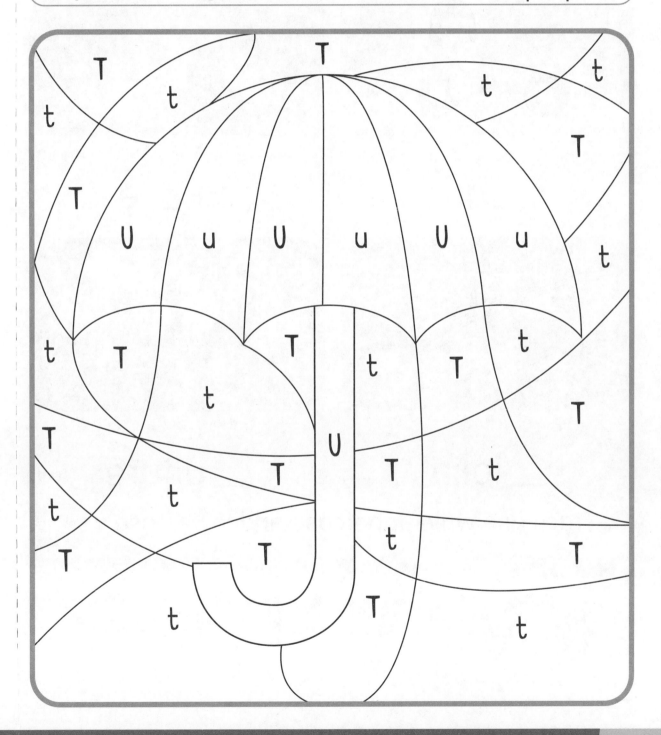

The Letter V

Write the missing **v**'s in these words.

__an   ca__e

__iolin   __ulture

Trace and write uppercase and lowercase **v**'s.

V is for Volcano

Search the silly scene for these things that start with **v**.
Check the boxes when you find them.

1 **v**olcano 2 **v**ets 3 **v**ases 4 **v**ests

The Letter W

Find and circle the words that start with **w**.
They can go across or down.

web

window

wolf

wand

z	l	q	i	p	d	n	o	i
i	g	l	t	t	e	z	w	k
k	j	t	w	i	v	w	a	b
d	m	a	e	f	k	l	n	e
n	a	a	b	j	f	y	d	n
h	p	l	o	c	r	h	l	g
e	o	w	i	n	d	o	w	f
w	p	m	g	e	h	g	b	m
s	c	n	w	o	l	f	i	u

Trace and write uppercase and lowercase **w**'s.

Ww Ww

Wendy's Warehouse

Wendy's **W**arehouse only sells things that start with **w**.
Circle the items **W**endy can sell in her **w**arehouse.
Put an X over the items **W**endy can't sell.

yo-yo

wagon

rope

watch

Wendy's Warehouse

hammer

wheel

paint

whistle

The Letter X

Trace the **x**'s with your finger. Then draw lines to match the words to the uppercase or lowercase letter.

fox

wax

Xena

Xavier

xylophone

six

Trace and write uppercase and lowercase **x**'s.

X Marks the Spot

Use the color key to reveal where the treasure is buried.

Key: X = red, v = green, T = orange, t = blue

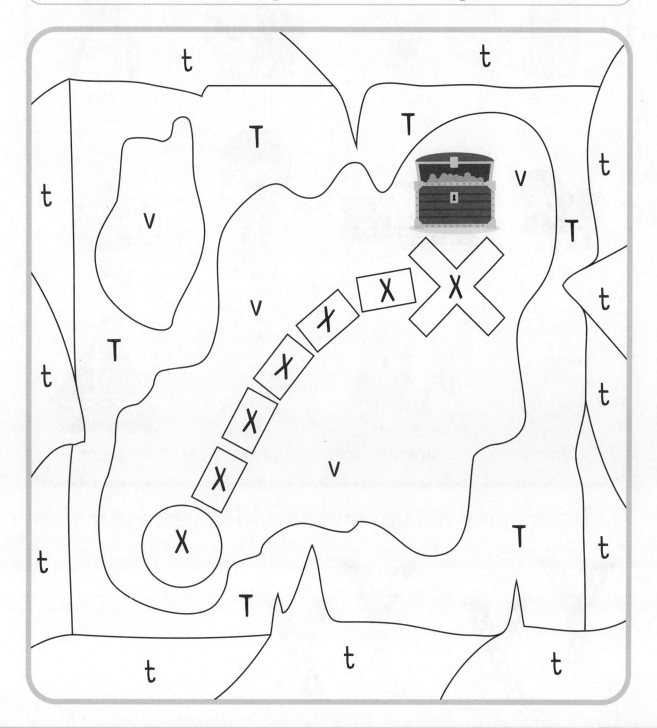

The Letter Y

Circle the things that start with **y**.

phone **y**ogurt **b**ear **c**hair

yak **t**rain **y**awn **s**lippers

yolk **u**nicorn **j**ewel **y**acht

Trace and write uppercase and lowercase **y**'s.

Yo-Yo Maze

Can you reach the uppercase **Y** inside the **y**ellow **y**o-**y**o?
Collect all the lowercase **y**'s along the way.

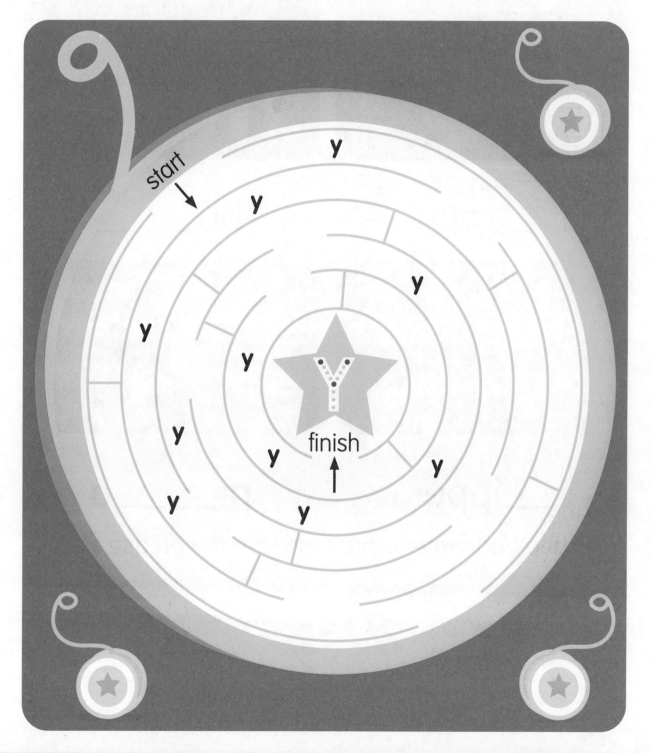

The Letter Z

Write the missing **z**'s in these words.

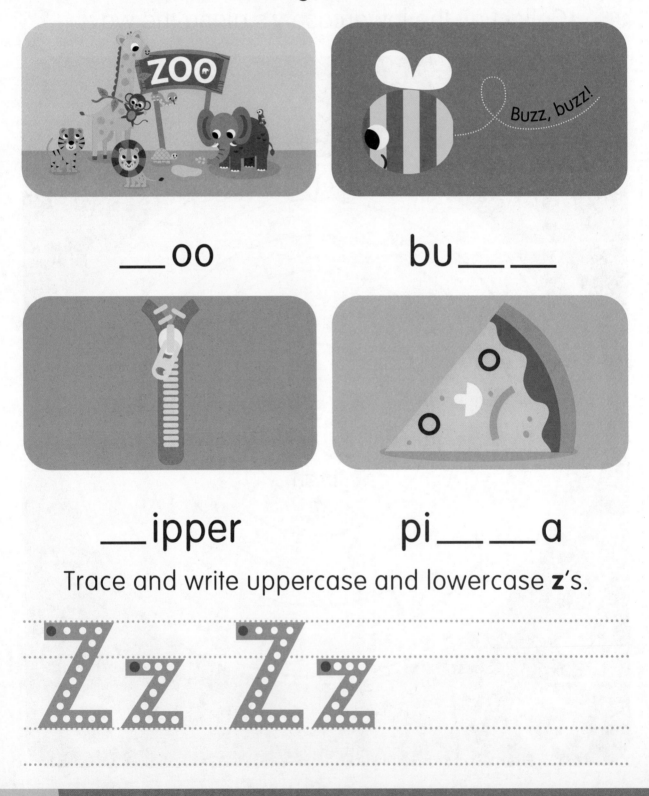

__ oo

bu__ __

__ipper

pi__ __a

Trace and write uppercase and lowercase **z**'s.

Zz Zz Zz

Zigzag Zebras

Find and point to 5 **z**ebras.
Then find and circle 5 **z**'s.

Alphabet City

Write the missing uppercase letters in alphabetical order.

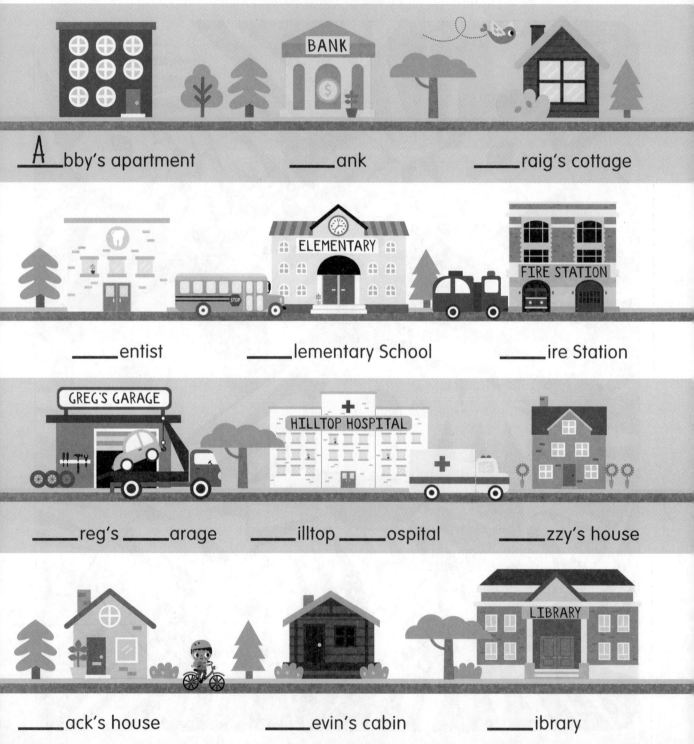

A bby's apartment   _____ank   _____raig's cottage

_____entist   _____lementary School   _____ire Station

_____reg's _____arage   _____illtop _____ospital   _____zzy's house

_____ack's house   _____evin's cabin   _____ibrary

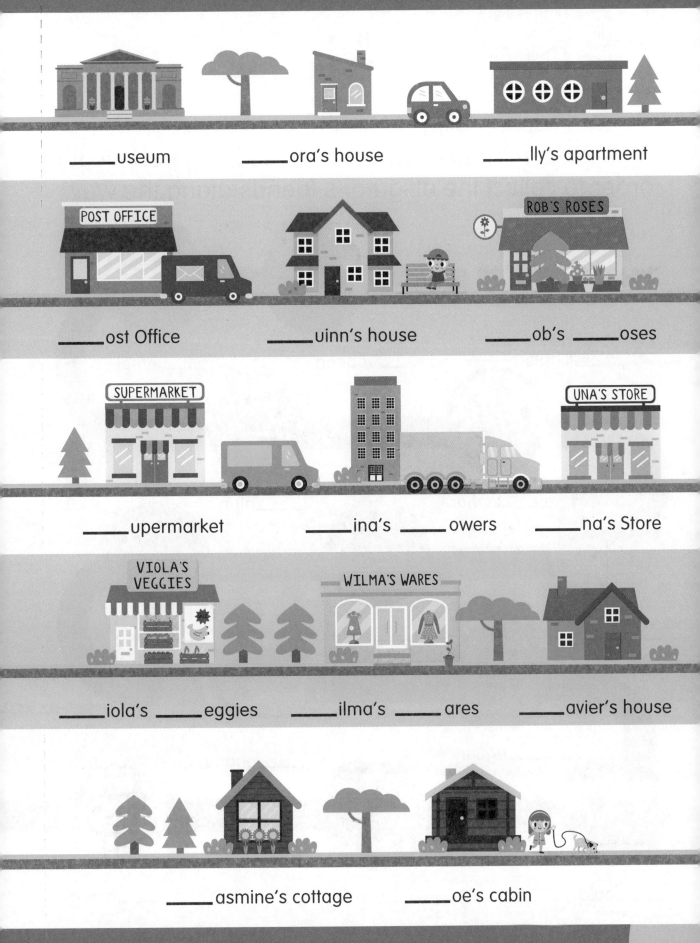

_____useum   _____ora's house   _____lly's apartment

_____ost Office   _____uinn's house   _____ob's _____oses

_____upermarket   _____ina's _____owers   _____na's Store

_____iola's _____eggies   _____ilma's _____ares   _____avier's house

_____asmine's cottage   _____oe's cabin

Animal Alphabet

Help the alligator get back to the zoo.
Write the missing lowercase letters in alphabetical
order to collect the alligator's friends along the way.

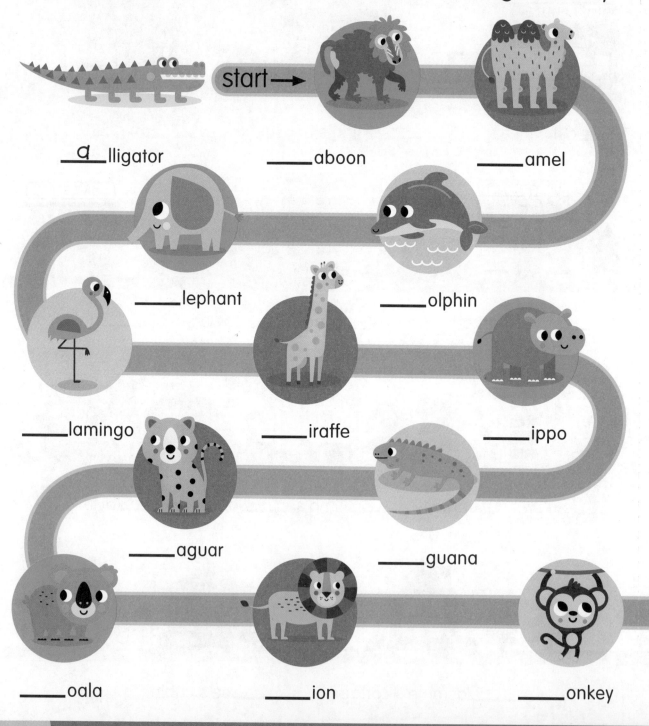

__a__lligator

_____aboon

_____amel

_____lephant

_____olphin

_____lamingo

_____iraffe

_____ippo

_____aguar

_____guana

_____oala

_____ion

_____onkey

_____arwhal

_____tter

_____enguin

_____eal

_____hino

_____uail

_____iger

_____rchin

_____ulture

fo _____

_____hale

ZOO

_____ak

_____oo

finish

Sh and Th

Say each word aloud and listen for the **sh** or **th sound**.
Then trace the letters that stand for the **sh** or **th sound**.

ship shop

bush fish

thumb 3 three

sloth moth

Leap Frog

Say each word aloud and listen for a **sh** or **th sound**.
Then color the lily pads with **sh** and **th** words.

start

ship

moth

three

shoe

sun

path

dog

bus

man

fish

cat

play

rush

thumb

hat

web

sloth

finish

Ch and Tch

Both **ch** and **tch** can stand for the **ch sound**.
Say each word aloud and listen for the **ch sound**.
Then match the word to the correct picture.

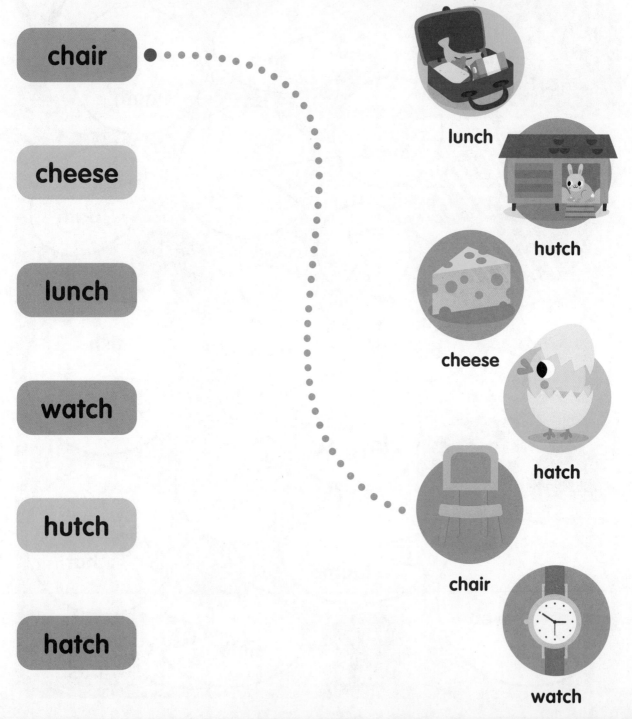

chair

cheese

lunch

watch

hutch

hatch

lunch

hutch

cheese

hatch

chair

watch

Quick Quiz

Look at the pictures and say each word aloud.

hatch

hutch

chair

cheese

lunch

Circle the two words that start with **ch** with a **green** pencil.

Circle the two words that end in **tch** with a **blue** pencil.

Circle the word that ends in **ch** with a **red** pencil.

Wh and Wr

Wr stands for the **r sound**, and **wh** stands for the **w sound**. Say each word and listen for the **r** or **w** sound. Then circle the letters to spell the word.

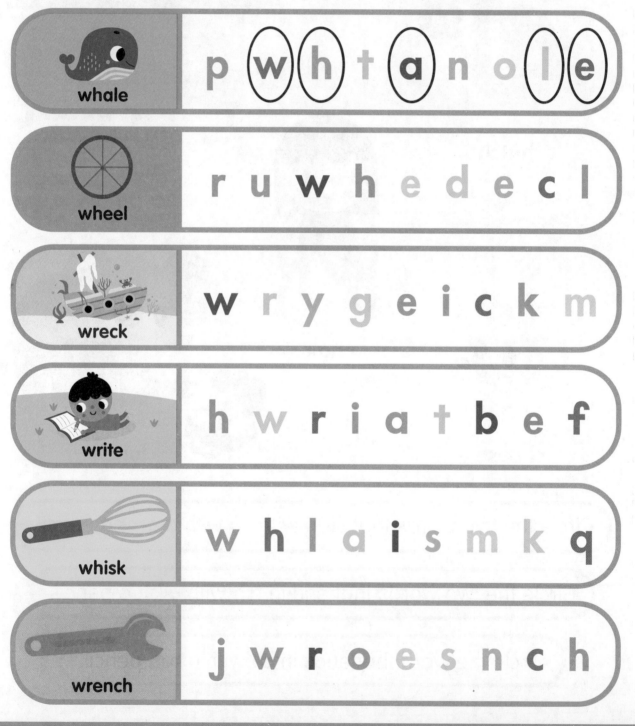

whale — p (w)(h) t (a) n o (l)(e)

wheel — r u **w** h e d e c l

wreck — **w** r y g e i c k m

write — h **w** **r** **i** a **t** b e f

whisk — **w** **h** l **a** **i** s m k q

wrench — j **w** **r** o e s n c h

Word Jam

Say each word aloud and listen for the **r** or **w sound**.
Color the **cars** with **wr** words **green**.
Color the **cars** with **wh** words **red**.

write

whale

wheel

wreck

whisk

wrench

wrap

when

Ph and Gh

Both **ph** and **gh** can stand for the **f sound**.
Say each word aloud and listen for the **f sound**.
Then match the word to the correct picture.

phone

photo

dolphin

trophy

laugh

cough

dolphin

Ha, ha!

laugh

photo

phone

cough

trophy

Secret Word Puzzle

Say each word below aloud and listen for the **f sound**. Then use the words to fill in the puzzle.

dolphin   **laugh**   **phone**   **cough**   **trophy**

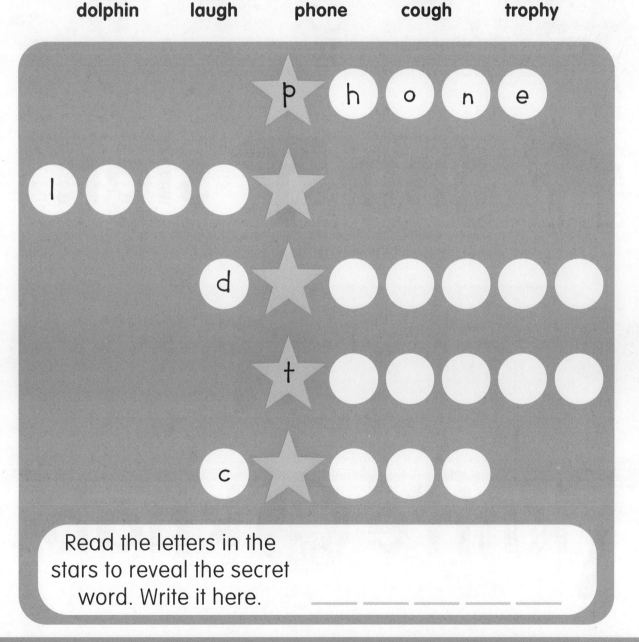

p ⭐ p h o n e

l ◯ ◯ ◯ ⭐

d ⭐ ◯ ◯ ◯ ◯ ◯

t ◯ ◯ ◯ ◯ ◯

c ⭐ ◯ ◯ ◯

Read the letters in the stars to reveal the secret word. Write it here. _ _ _ _ _

Gn and Kn

Both **gn** and **kn** can stand for the **n sound**.
Say each word aloud and listen for the **n sound**.
Then trace the letters that make the **n sound**.

Bunny Hops

Trace the bunnies' hops and say each sound as you land on it. Then blend the sounds to make a word.

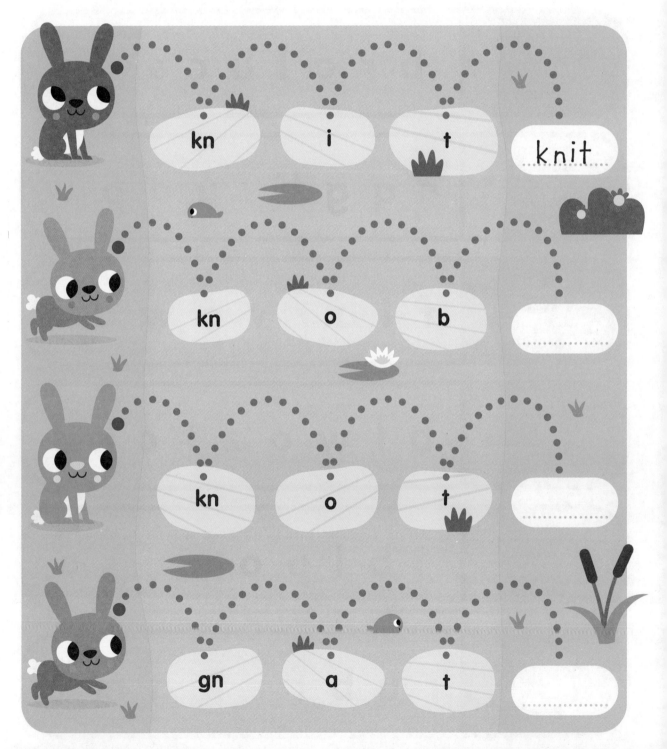

kn · i · t → knit

kn · o · b →

kn · o · t →

gn · a · t →

Br and Bl

Say each word aloud and listen for the **br** or **bl sound**.
Then circle the letters to spell the word.

brush

b r o l u c s n h

blow

c q g b l u o p w

brown

f i b r v o w d n

blocks

b l w o z t c k s

blouse

i b l p o u q s e

bread

r u b r e k a m d

Dino Dash

Say each word aloud and listen for a **br** or **bl sound**. Then color the rocks with **br** and **bl** words to help the dinosaur cross the lava.

start

watch

bath

brush

brown

blow

dress

knit

phone

blog

blocks

net

pen

bread

cup

dot

top

shop

brag

wheel

blouse

wreck

not

ten

finish

Nk and Ng

The letters **ng** can stand for the **ng sound**, and the letters **nk** can stand for the **ng** and **k sounds** put together. Say each word aloud and color **ng** or **nk**.

ri**ng**

go**ng**

ba**ng**

swi**ng**

si**nk**

ba**nk**

Treasure Chests

Fill the **red** treasure chest with words that have the **ng sound**. Fill the **blue** treasure chest with words that have the **ng** and **k sounds**.

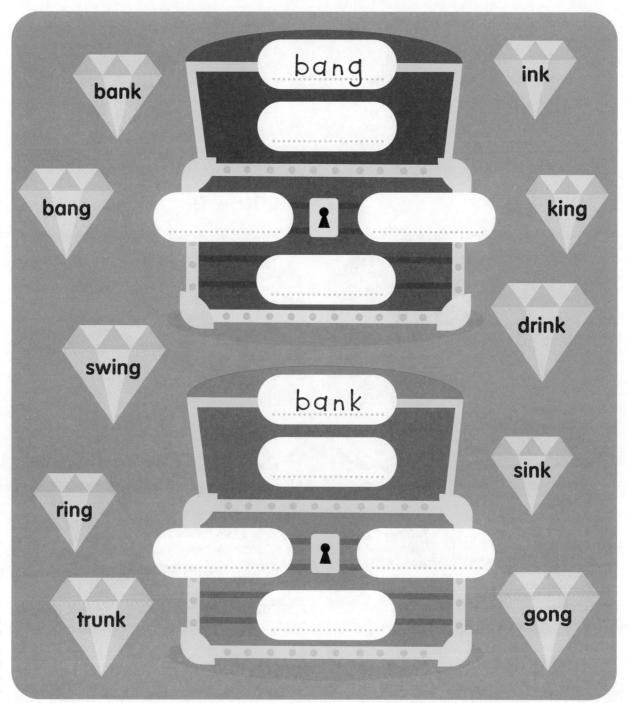

Silent E

A **silent e** makes the vowel say its name. Add an **e** to end of these words to make new words. Then say each word aloud and listen for the **vowel sound**.

pin + e = ...

cap + e = ...

kit + e = ...

tub + e = ...

not + e = ...

plan + e = ...

Buzzy Bee

Say each word aloud and listen for the **vowel sound**. Then color the flowers with **silent e** words to help the bee reach the hive.

Long A Sound

Say each word aloud and listen for the **long a sound**.
Then trace the letters that stand for the **long a sound**.

baby   lady

jay   play

rain   snail

cake   wave

Blast Off!

Write the letters that stand for the **long a sound** in each word. Then say the word aloud.

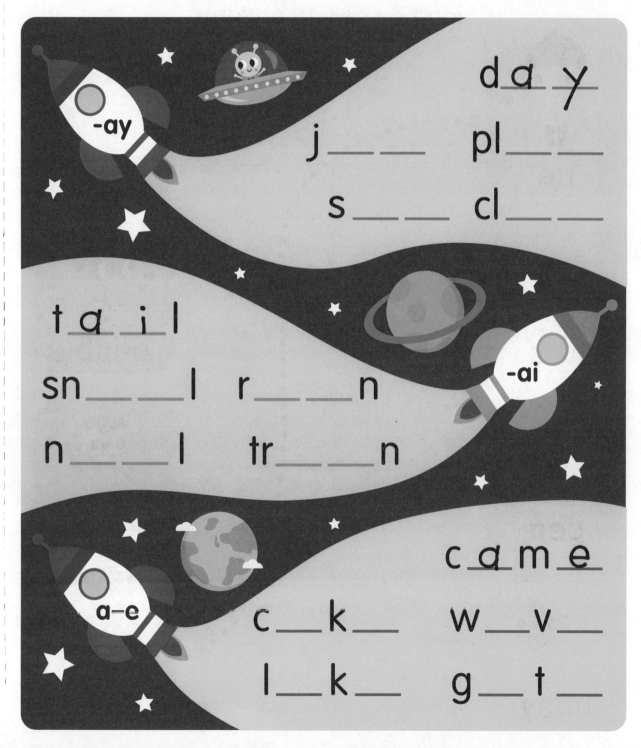

-ay

d a y

j ___ ___   pl ___ ___

s ___ ___   cl ___ ___

t a i l

sn ___ ___ l   r ___ ___ n

n ___ ___ l   tr ___ ___ n

-ai

c a m e

c ___ k ___   w ___ v ___

l ___ k ___   g ___ t ___

a-e

Long E Sound

Say each word aloud and listen for the **long e sound**. Then draw lines to link the words with the same **long e** spelling patterns.

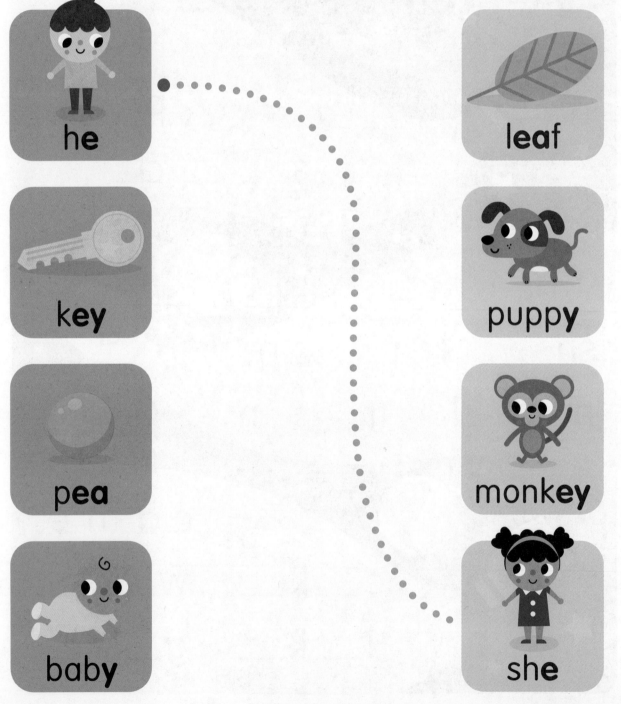

he

leaf

key

puppy

pea

monkey

baby

she

Monkey Swings

Trace the monkeys' swings, and say each sound as you land on it. Then blend the sounds to make a word.

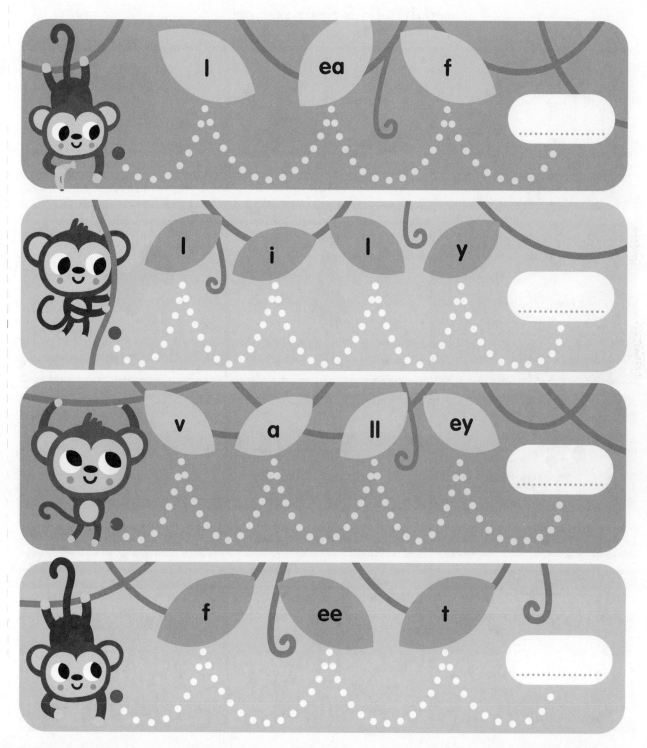

l ea f

l i l y

v a ll ey

f ee t

Long I Sound

In each row, say the first word aloud and listen for the **long i sound**. Then circle the word that **rhymes** with the first word.

bike	dig	hike
pie	tie	pin
fly	bib	cry
light	king	knight

Circle the Word

Name each picture aloud and listen for the **vowel sound**. Then circle the word that matches the picture.

pin   pie

bike   big

knight   knit

fin   fly

lime   lint

fist   five

Long O Sound

Say each word aloud and listen for the **long o sound**. Then draw lines to link the words with the same **long o** spelling patterns.

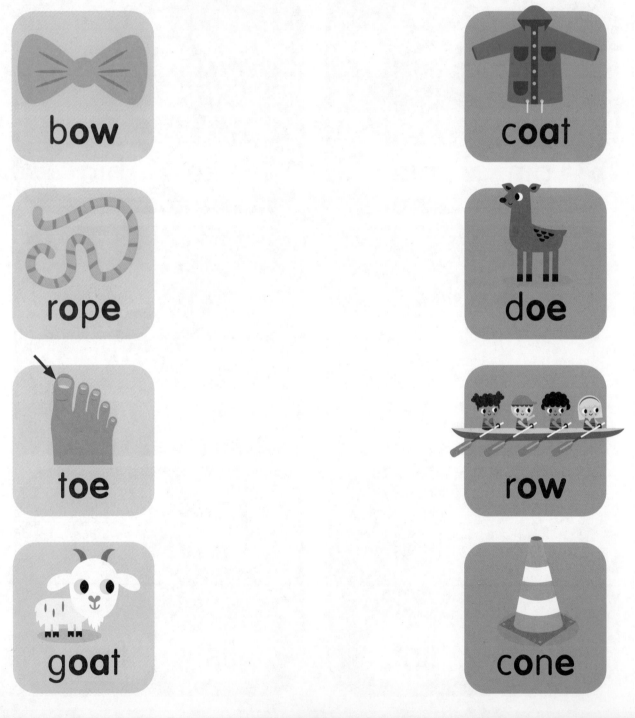

bow

coat

rope

doe

toe

row

goat

cone

Cute Caterpillars

Write the letters that stand for the **long o sound** in each word. Then say the word aloud.

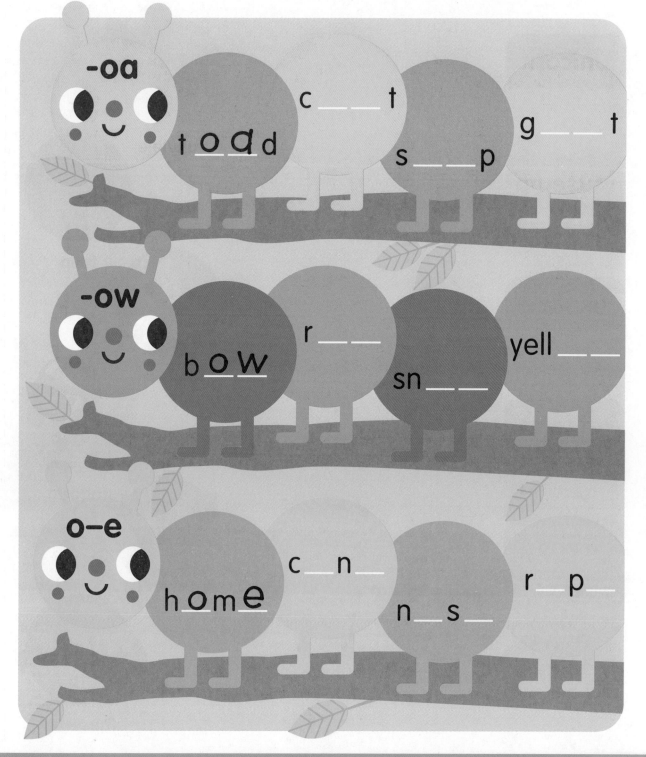

-oa

t o a d

c _ _ t

s _ _ _ p

g _ _ _ t

-ow

b o w

r _ _ _

sn _ _ _

yell _ _ _

o–e

h o m e

c _ n _

n _ s _

r _ p _

Long U Sound

Say each word aloud and listen for the **long u sound**.
Then match the word to the correct picture.

unicorn

museum

ukulele

uniform

ruby

tulip

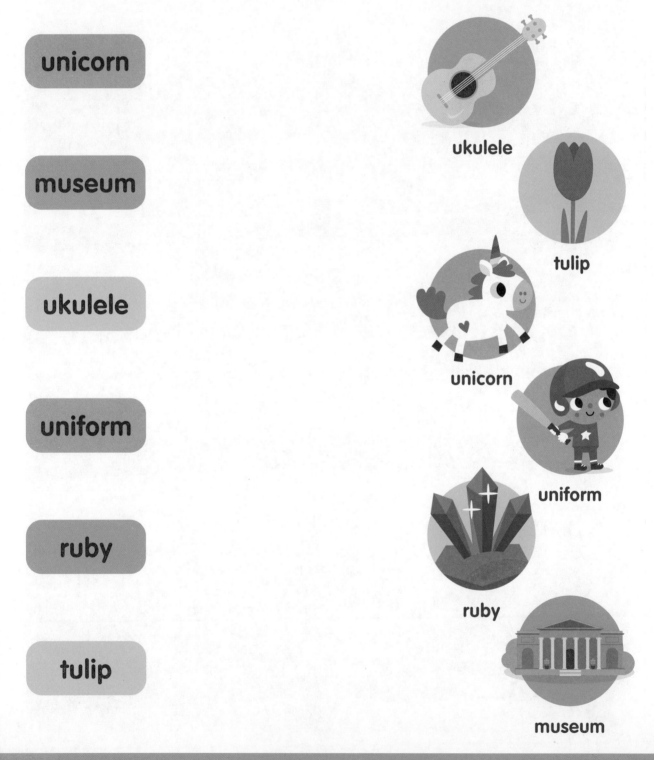

ukulele

tulip

unicorn

uniform

ruby

museum

Label It!

Say each word aloud and listen for the **long u sound**.
Then label the pictures using the words.

unicorn   ukulele   uniform   tulip   ruby   museum

Bossy R Words

When **r** comes after a **vowel**, it changes the **vowel sound**. Say the words and listen for the **vowel sound**. Then trace the letters that make the **vowel sound**.

car shark

fern corn

skirt girl

nurse surf

Missing Sounds

Name each picture aloud and listen for the **vowel sound**. Then fill in the **vowel sound** in the middle of the word.

sh___ ___k

g___ ___l

c___ ___n

c___ ___

n___ ___se

f___ ___n

Oi Sound

Say each word aloud and listen for the **oi sound**.
Then circle the letters to spell the word.

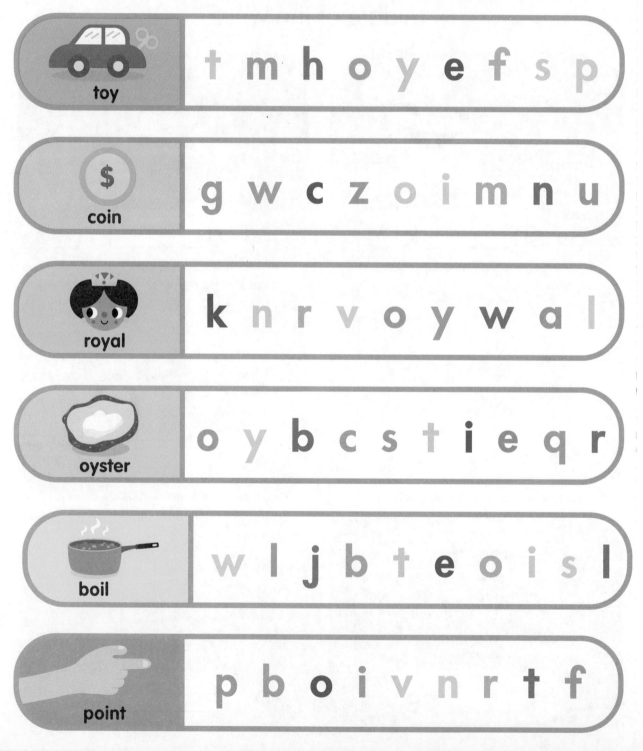

toy — t m h o y e f s p

coin — g w c z o i m n u

royal — k n r v o y w a l

oyster — o y b c s t i e q r

boil — w l j b t e o i s l

point — p b o i v n r t f

Let's Go Fishing!

Fill the **green** bucket with words that contain the **oy spelling pattern**. Fill the **orange** bucket with words that contain the **oi spelling pattern**.

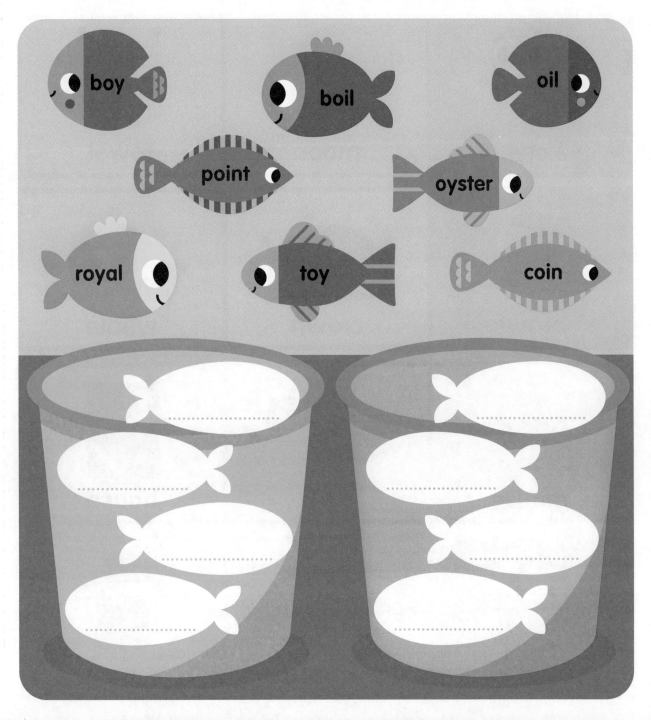

Ou Sound

In each row, say the first word aloud and listen for the **ou sound**. Then circle the word that **rhymes** with the first word.

owl	moon	towel
brown	crown	whale
mouse	cake	house
shout	trout	coat

Link the Sounds

Follow the beads and write the words. Then say each word aloud and listen for the **ou sound**.

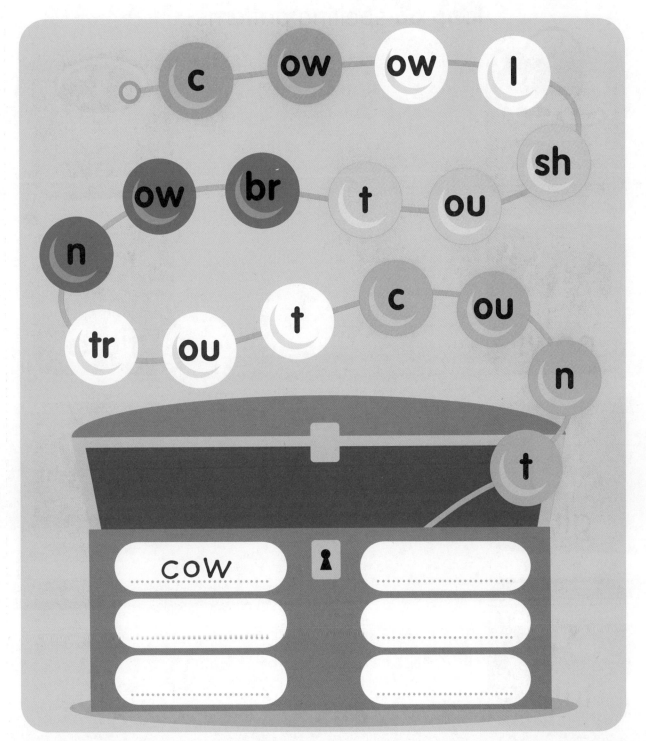

cow

Long Oo Sound

Say each word aloud and listen for the **long oo sound**. Then draw lines to link the words with the same **long oo** spelling patterns.

food

newt

glue

tube

st**ew**

fl**ute**

bab**oo**n

stat**ue**

Sweet Tooth

Say **moon**. Color the **candies** with this **long oo** sound **orange**. Say **hook**. Color the **candies** with this **short oo** sound **pink**.

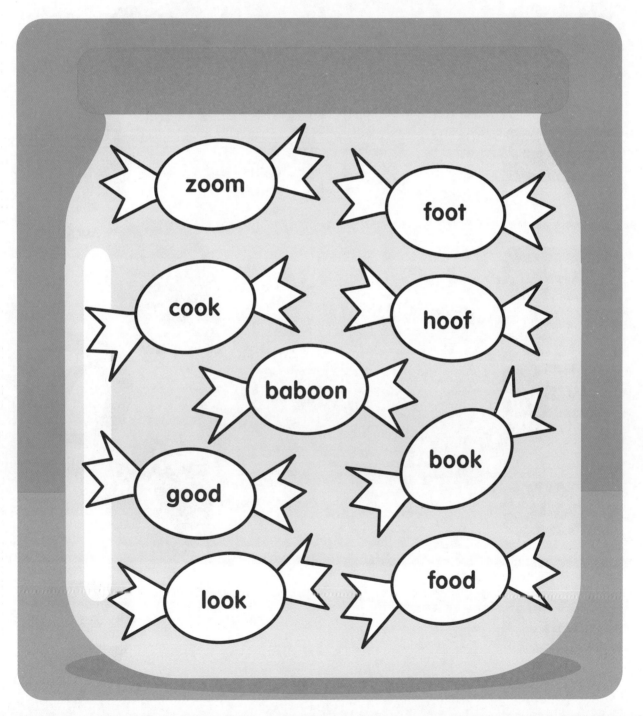

Aw Sound

Say each word aloud and listen for the **aw sound**.
Then match the word to the correct picture.

paw

yawn

hawk

wall

ball

fall

fall

wall

paw

ball

hawk

yawn

Picture This!

Say each word aloud and listen for the **aw sound**.
Then label the pictures using the words.

paw   wall   yawn   hawk   fall   ball

Air Sound

In each row, say the first word aloud and listen for the **air sound**. Then circle the word that **rhymes** with the first word.

chair	hair	shoe
bear	pear	boat
hare	star	square
fairy	dairy	cookie

Up, Up, and Away!

Write the letters that stand for the **air sound** in each word. Then say the word aloud.

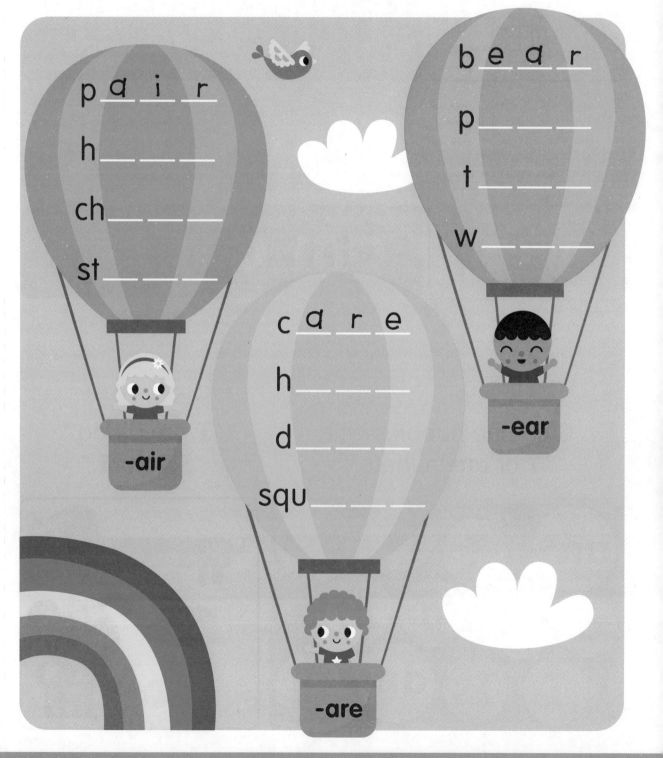

p <u>a i r</u>

h <u>_____</u>

ch<u>_____</u>

st<u>_____</u>

-air

c <u>a r e</u>

h <u>_____</u>

d <u>_____</u>

squ<u>_____</u>

-are

b <u>e a r</u>

p <u>_____</u>

t <u>_____</u>

w <u>_____</u>

-ear

I and am

Read it, color it, trace it, and write it.

I   I I I I I

am   am am am

Color the bubbles with
I or **am** in them.

"**I am** a dog."
"So **am I**."

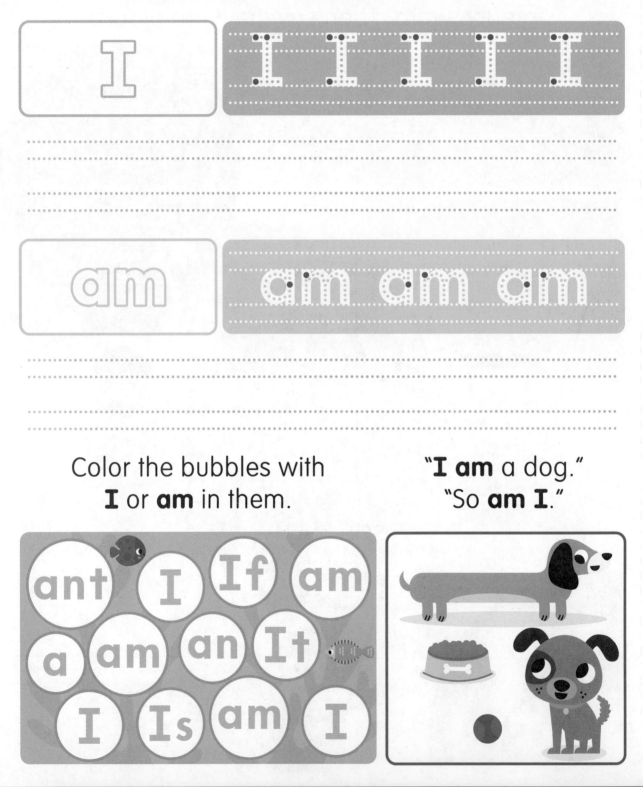

a and an

Read it, color it, trace it, and write it.

a   a a a a a

....
....
....

an   an an an

....
....
....

Is it **an** ant
or **a** bee?

Circle each **a** in yellow, and
circle each **an** in pink.

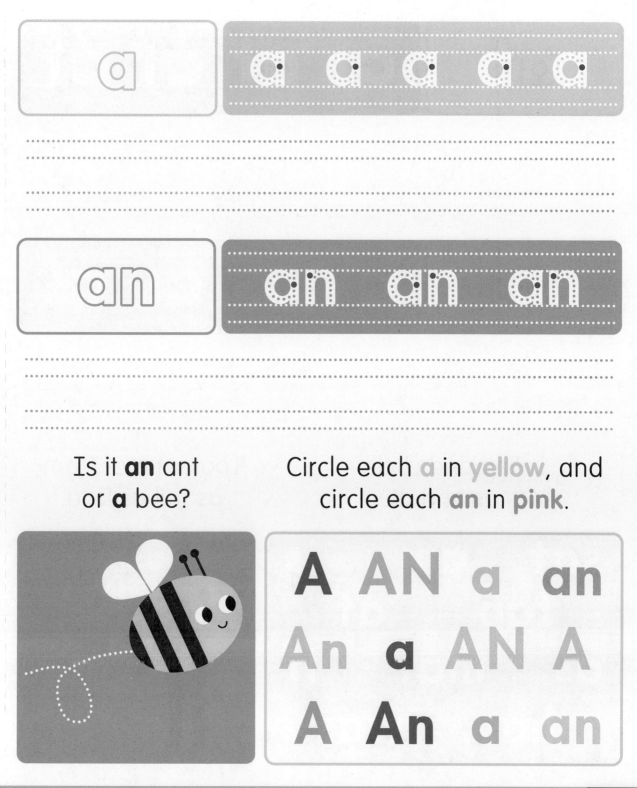

A AN a an
An a AN A
A An a an

at and as

Read it, color it, trace it, and write it.

at | at at at at

as | as as as as

Find and circle as and at.

sat am is
tap at
as mat it
has was

Look at me! I am as tall as Dad.

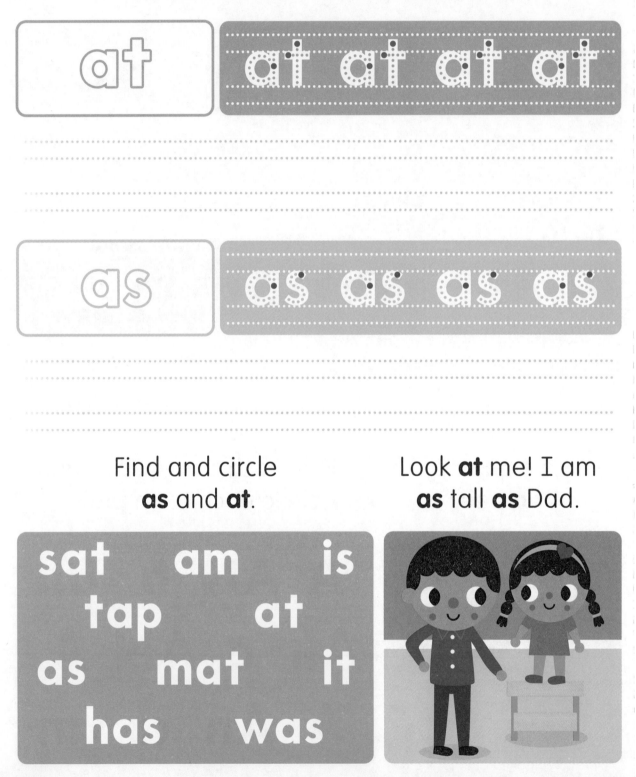

is and it

Read it, color it, trace it, and write it.

is is is is is is

it it it it it it

What **is it**?
It is an alien!

Trace and write
the sight words.

It is a cat.

_____ a fish.

he and she

Read it, color it, trace it, and write it.

he | he   he   he

she | she she she

Find and circle **he** or **she** in each word.

He is five, and **she** is six.

here   heel
sheen   heap
hero   sheep
sheet

we and me

Read it, color it, trace it, and write it.

| we | we we we |

| me | me me me |

"**We** like cats."
"**Me**, too!"

Use the key to color in.
Key: **we = blue**, **me = yellow**

we we
we
me me
we
we me
me
me me
we me me
we we
we we

103

be and see

Read it, color it, trace it, and write it.

be | be be be

see | see see see

Find and circle **be** and **see**.

He will **be** happy to **see** you.

been   be
sea   she
he   we
me   see

by and my

Read it, color it, trace it, and write it.

by by by by

....
....
....

my my my my

....
....
....

My house is
by a river.

Join the **by**'s to the **b**
and the **my**'s to the **m**.

do and to

Read it, color it, trace it, and write it.

| do | do   do   do |

| to | to   to   to |

Color the bubbles with
do or **to** in them.

I **do** this **to**
keep fit.

got   to   go

do   to   do

too   do   dot

up and us

Read it, color it, trace it, and write it.

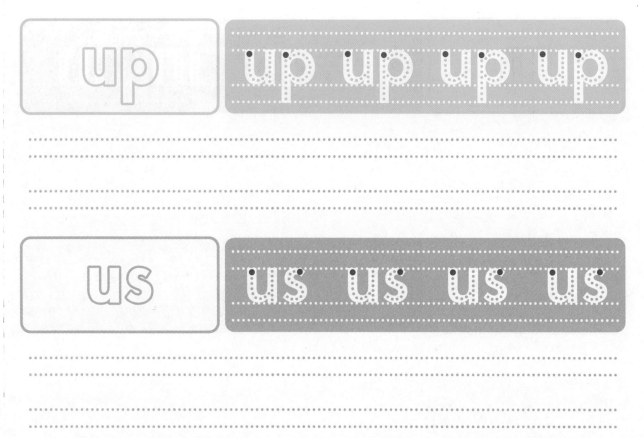

He climbs **up**
to see **us**.

Circle each **up** in **yellow**,
and circle each **us** in **purple**.

us	UP	Us	up
US	up	us	Up
Us	UP	US	up

in and if

Read it, color it, trace it, and write it.

in | in in in in

if | if if if if

Find and circle **in** and **if**.

If it is hot, we will swim **in** the pool.

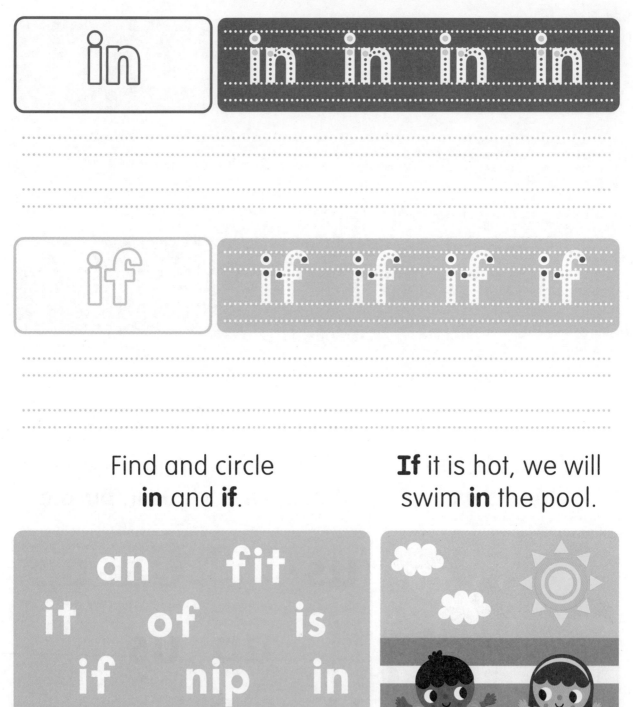

an fit
it of is
if nip in
on into

on and off

Read it, color it, trace it, and write it.

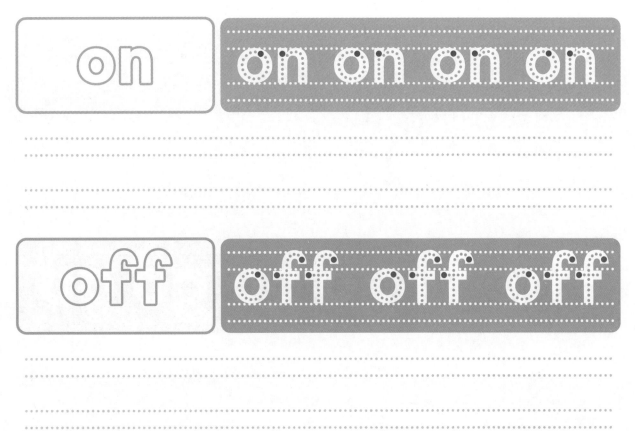

I get **on** at home.
I get **off** at school.

Write **on** by the lamp that is **on**.
Write **off** by the lamp that is **off**.

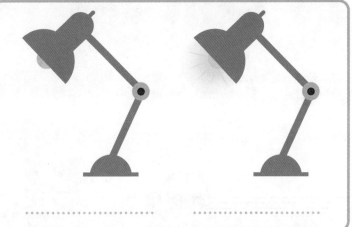

so and go

Read it, color it, trace it, and write it.

so | so so so so

go | go go go go

Trace the sight words.

It can go so fast.

It is **so** windy I have to **go** home.

and and did

Read it, color it, trace it, and write it.

and · and · and ·

did did did

"What **did** you see?"
"A dog **and** a frog!"

Find and circle **and** or **did** in each word.

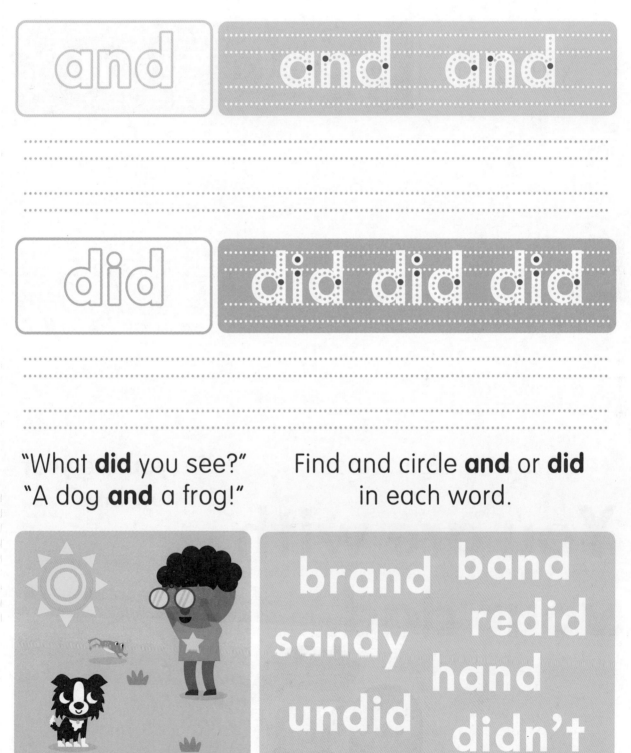

brand band
sandy redid
hand
undid didn't

you and your

Read it, color it, trace it, and write it.

you   you   you

your   your   your

Trace the sight words.

"Do **you** like **your** new bike?"

You are with your dad.

want and went

Read it, color it, trace it, and write it.

want   want want

went   went   went

I **went** skiing, and
I **want** to go again.

Use the key to color the words.
Key: **a = green**, **e = blue**,
n = red, **t = orange**, **w = pink**

went
want

our and out

Read it, color it, trace it, and write it.

our | our our our

out | out out out

Find and circle **our** or **out** in each word.

My hat fell **out** of **our** boat.

scout sour
hour shout
about flour
outside

now and how

Read it, color it, trace it, and write it.

now | now now

how | how how

How now brown cow?

Circle the words that rhyme with **now** and **how**.

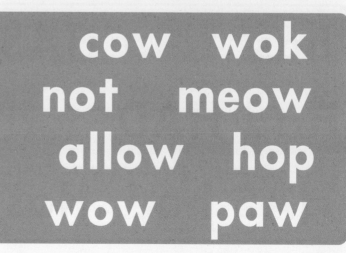

cow wok
not meow
allow hop
wow paw

has and had

Read it, color it, trace it, and write it.

has | has has has

had | had had had

Circle each **has** in **blue**, and circle each **had** in **yellow**.

has	Had	HAS
Had	**HAD**	had
HAS	had	**Has**

She **has had** a dance class today.

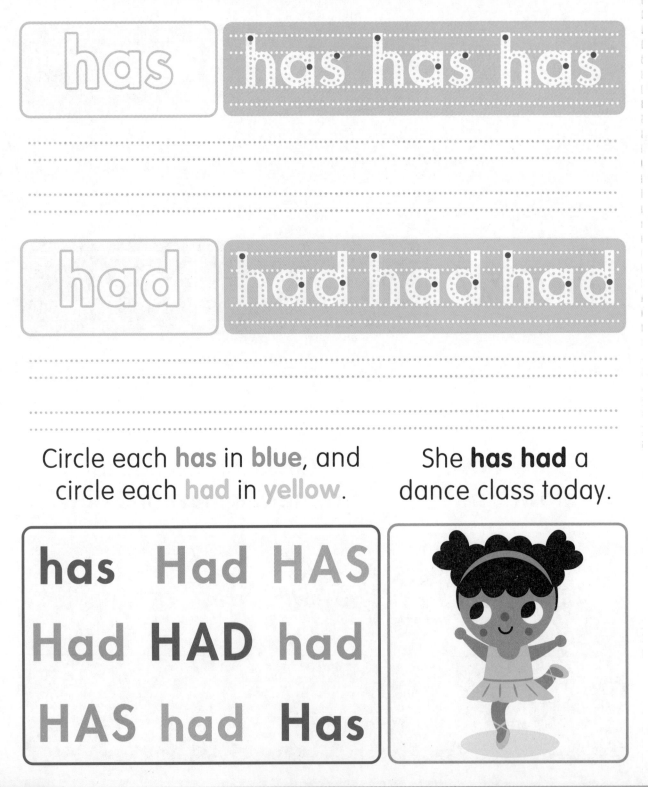

are and were

Read it, color it, trace it, and write it.

are | are are are

were | were were

There **were** 3 cupcakes. Now there **are** 2.

Use the key to color in.
Key: **are = green**, **were = red**

were
were
are
were
were
were
are
are
are
are
are
were
are
were
were
are
were
were
were
were
were

can and ran

Read it, color it, trace it, and write it.

| can | can can can |

| ran | ran ran ran |

Circle the words that rhyme with **can** and **ran**.

They **ran** fast.
Can you run fast?

pan   man
rat   run
cap   fan
tan   ram

too and soon

Read it, color it, trace it, and write it.

too | too   too

soon | soon   soon

"I hope our food comes **soon**."
"Me, **too**!"

Find and circle **too** and **soon**.

to   two
tow   soon
moon   too
tool   soot

for and from

Read it, color it, trace it, and write it.

for | for for for

from | from from

Circle each **for** in **red**, and circle each from in yellow.

"This is **for** you. It is **from** Grandpa."

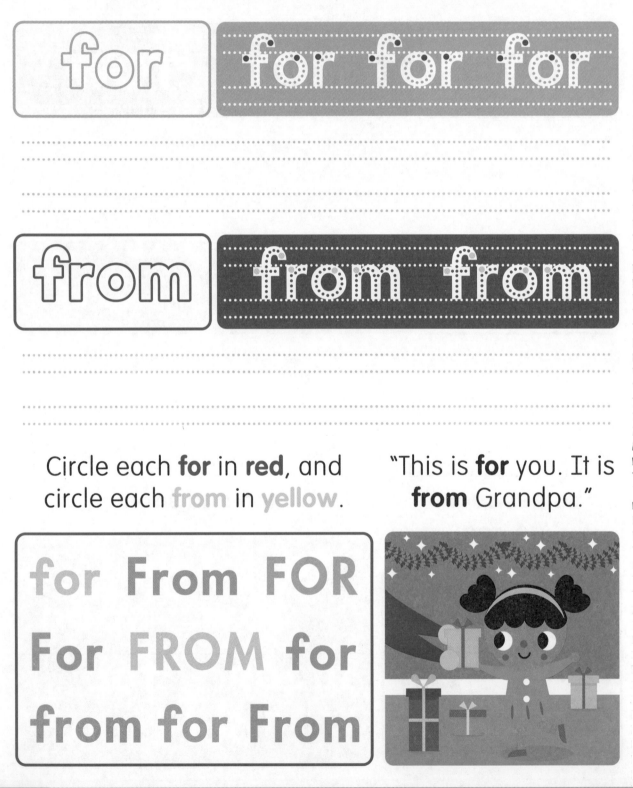

for From FOR
For FROM for
from for From

make and came

Read it, color it, trace it, and write it.

make · make make

....

....

came · came came

....

....

Grandpa **came** over to **make** us a cake.

Match each word to the sight word it rhymes with.

flame

rake

make

came

cake

frame

come and some

Read it, color it, trace it, and write it.

come | come come

some | some some

Find and circle **come** and **some**.

cone   come
sum   become
came   some
sole   same

Come and have **some** cookies!

like and look

Read it, color it, trace it, and write it.

like · like · like

look · look · look

Look at my hair. Do you **like** the color?

Use the key to color the words. Key: **k = green**, **l = blue**, **i = red**, **o = orange**, **e = pink**

like
look

any and only

Read it, color it, trace it, and write it.

any | any any any

only | only only

Color the bubbles with **any** or **only** in them.

only   ant   many   any   lonely   one   only   any

"Did you pick **any** berries?"
"**Only** one!"

but and must

Read it, color it, trace it, and write it.

but | but but

must | must must

We are having fun, **but** we **must** go in soon.

Use the key to color in.
Key: **but = orange**, **must = yellow**

say and said

Read it, color it, trace it, and write it.

say | say say say

said | said said

Circle each **say** in **green**, and circle each **said** in **red**.

Dad **said** to pick apples, but he didn't **say** how many.

say Said SAY

Said SAID say

SAY said Say

will and with

Read it, color it, trace it, and write it.

will   will   will

with   with   with

"**Will** you play **with** me?"

Find and circle **will** and **with**.

wool   pith

will   wilt

well   wish

mill   with

more and most

Read it, color it, trace it, and write it.

more   more   more

most   most   most

Match each word to the sight word it rhymes with.

He is **more** colorful than **most** pigs.

door   toast

more

most

ghost   four

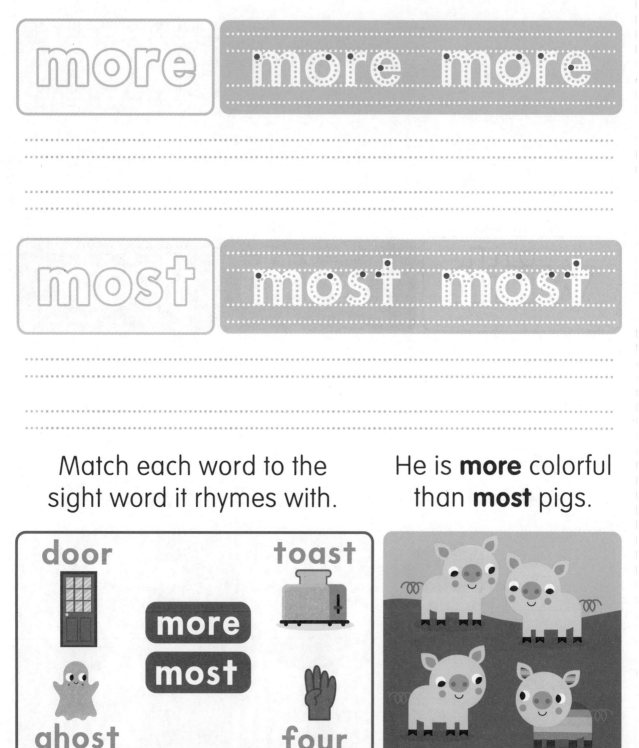

all and also

Read it, color it, trace it, and write it.

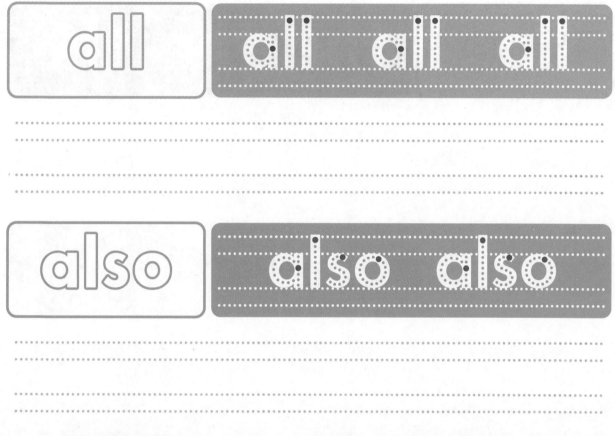

all   all   all   all

also   also   also

I like **all** sports.
I **also** like books.

Color the bubbles with
all or **also** in them.

also   all   ill   all
tall   at   almost
also

the and that

Read it, color it, trace it, and write it.

| the | the the the |

| that | that that |

Use the key to color the words.
Key: **h = green**, **t = blue**,
e = red, **a = orange**

That is **the** hat for me.

the
that

they and them

Read it, color it, trace it, and write it.

they · · · they · · they

· ·

· ·

them · · · them · them

· ·

· ·

They are our friends. We live next to **them**.

Join the **them**'s to the **m** and the **they**'s to the **y**.

they		them
they	**m**	they
	y	
them		them

131

this and their

Read it, color it, trace it, and write it.

this · this · this

their · their · their

Use the key to color the words.
Key: **th = blue**, **s = green**,
e = pink, i = orange, **r = red**

"Is **this their** spaceship?"

this
their

who and what

Read it, color it, trace it, and write it.

"**Who** are you?
What is your name?"

Find and circle
who and **what**.

where   who
while   why
what   whale
wheel   when

when and which

Read it, color it, trace it, and write it.

when | when when

which | which which

Circle each **when** in **red**, and circle each **which** in **blue**.

WHICH	When
WHEN	which
Which	WHEN
when	Which

Which movie are they going to? **When** does it start?

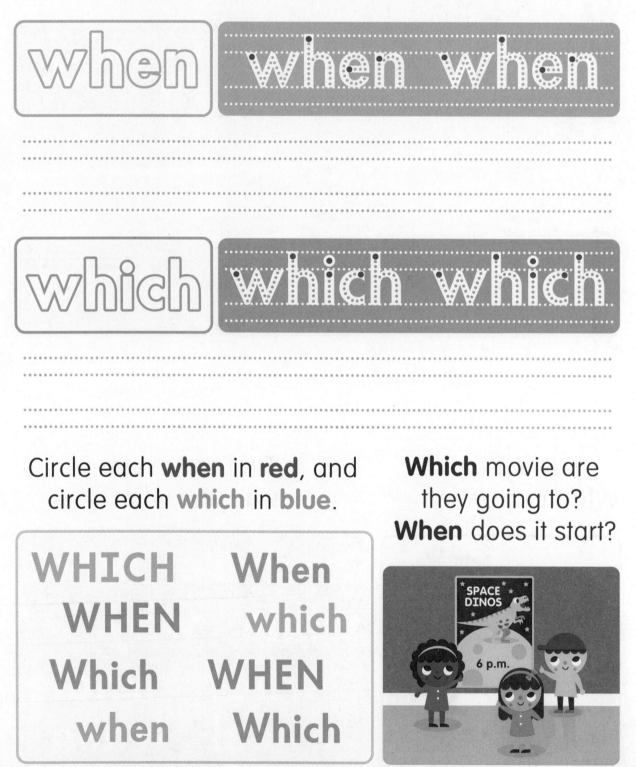

SPACE DINOS

6 p.m.

134

where and there

Read it, color it, trace it, and write it.

| where | where where |

| there | there there |

Where is our cat?
Oh, **there** she is!

Use the key to color the words.
Key: **e = green**, **r = blue**,
h = red, **t = purple**, **w = pink**

where
there

Let's Play!

Trace the **toy** words. Then match each word to the correct picture.

doll   bike

kite   ball

Spell it.

d·o·l·l

b·i·k·e

k·i·t·e

b·a·l·l

Color it.

doll

bike

kite

ball

Write it.

At School

Find and circle these things in the picture. Then **spell** each word aloud, **cover** it, and **write** it on the line.

table

bag

book

mat

Spell it.

b·o·o·k b·a·g
t·a·b·l·e m·a·t

Clap it.

b·o·o·k b·a·g
t·a·b·l·e m·a·t

Shout it!

b·o·o·k
b·a·g
t·a·b·l·e
m·a·t

Animal Letter Links

Trace the **animal** words.

cow   pig

bear   lion

Now find and link the letters to spell
the **animal** words.

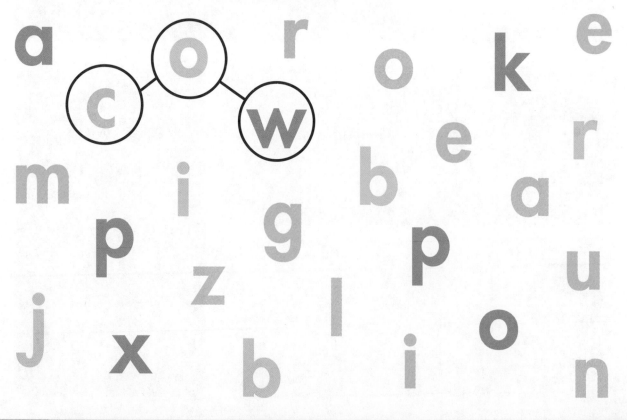

a   c   o   r   o   k   e

c   o   w   e

m   i   b   e   r

p   g   p   a

z   u

j   l   i   o

x   b   n

Code Breakers

Use the chart to break the codes
and spell the **animal** words.

a b c d e f g h i j k l m

n o p q r s t u v w x y z

p i g

_ _ _ _

_ _ _

_ _ _ _

Clap it.

**c·o·w   p·i·g
l·i·o·n   b·e·a·r**

Spell it.

**c·o·w   p·i·g
l·i·o·n   b·e·a·r**

Shout it!

**c·o·w   p·i·g
l·i·o·n   b·e·a·r**

Let's Go Shopping

Spell the **food** words three ways to finish the shopping list.

Trace it.

Write it yourself.

Write it in **rainbow** letters.

milk

rice

cake

eggs

plum

pizza

Family Maze

Help the **family** get home. As you pass each person,
spell the word aloud, cover it, and write it below.

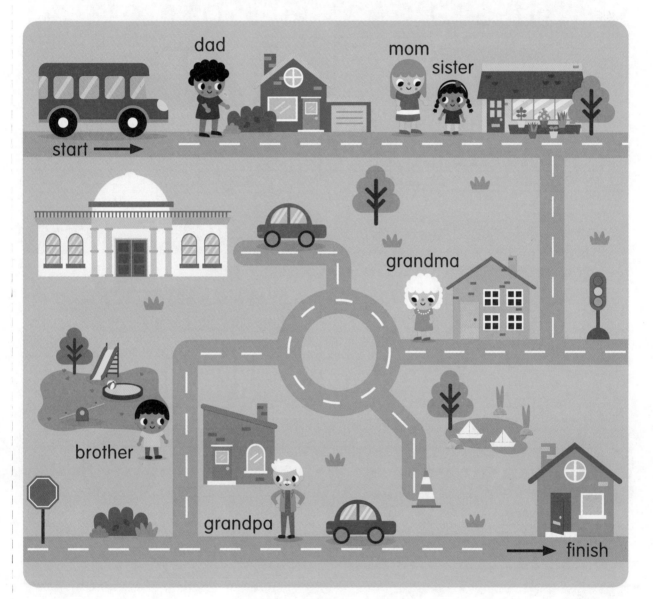

dad

On the Move

Unscramble the letters to spell the **vehicle** words.

u s b

a r c

n a v

s h p i

Spell it.
c·a·r v·a·n
s·h·i·p b·u·s

Clap it.
c·a·r v·a·n
s·h·i·p b·u·s

Sing it.
c·a·r
v·a·n
s·h·i·p
b·u·s

Roll and Race

Trace the words. Then play a game of **roll** and **race**.

How to Play

1 Roll a dice.

2 Find the lane that matches your roll.
   If you rolled a 5 or a 6, roll again.

3 Cover and write the word on the next empty line.

4 Keep rolling until all the words reach the finish.

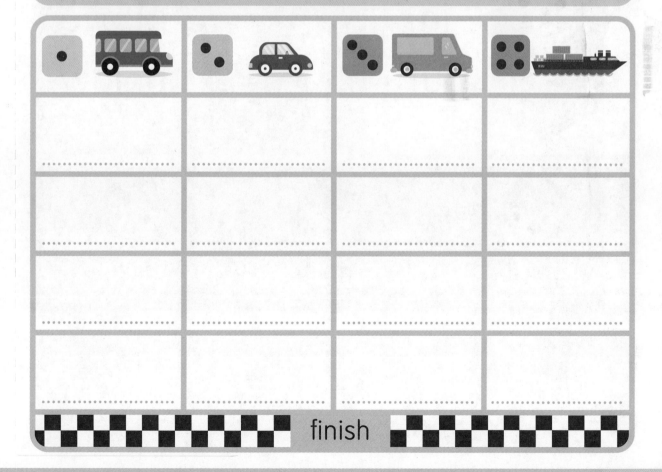

finish

Where Is It?

Circle the word that **matches** each picture.

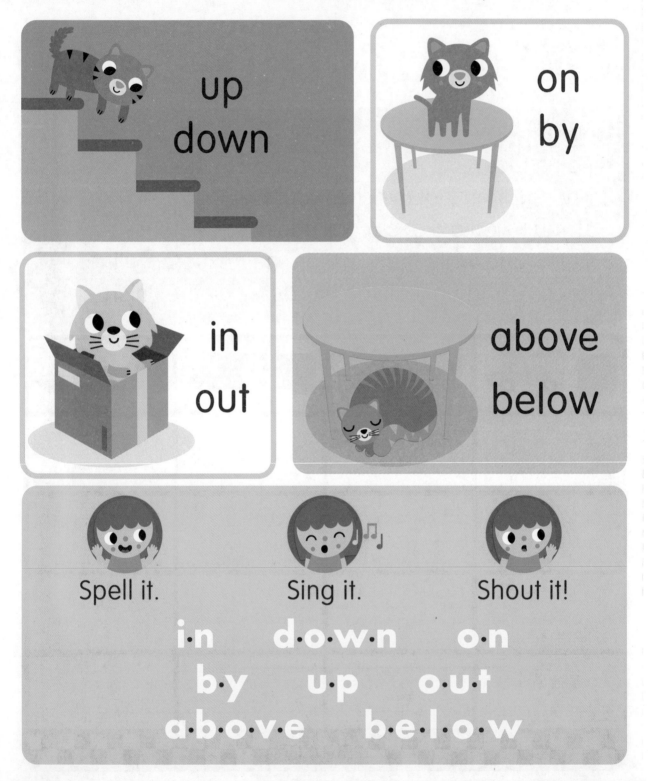

up
down

on
by

in
out

above
below

Spell it.   Sing it.   Shout it!

in   down   on
by   up   out
above   below

Find the Difference

Find and circle 4 **differences** between the pictures.
Cover and spell each **bold** word aloud as you find it.

Ladder Rhymes

Change the first letter of each word to make new **rhymes**.
Use the words in the box and the pictures to help you.

> hat   wig   ten   men   fig
> bat   rat   pen   dig

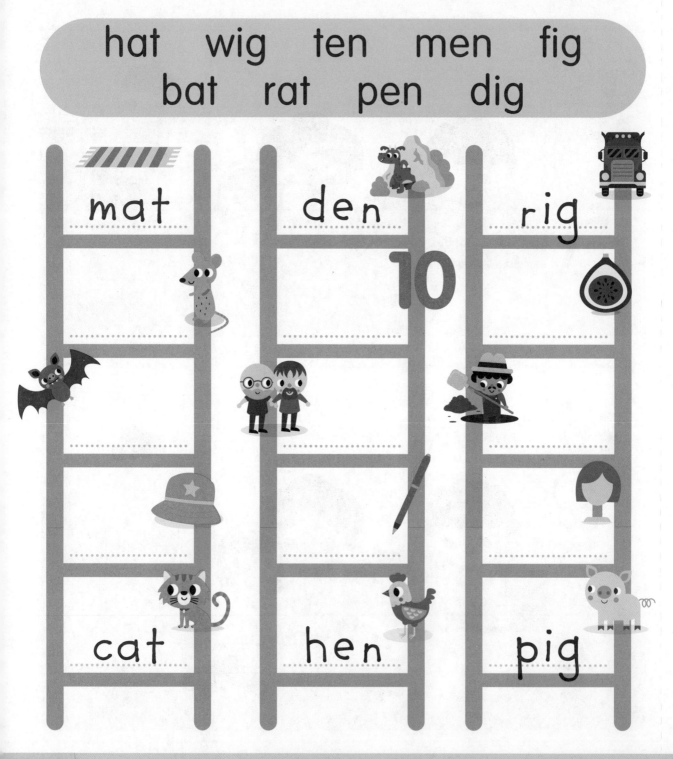

mat

den

rig

10

cat

hen

pig

Tic, Tac, Toe

Use the grid to play **Tic, Tac, Toe** with a friend.

How to Play
1 Each choose a word from the same rhyming pair.
2 Take turns writing your word in a box. Use a pencil.
3 The winner is the first one to get three words in a row.
4 Erase the words, and play again with a different pair.

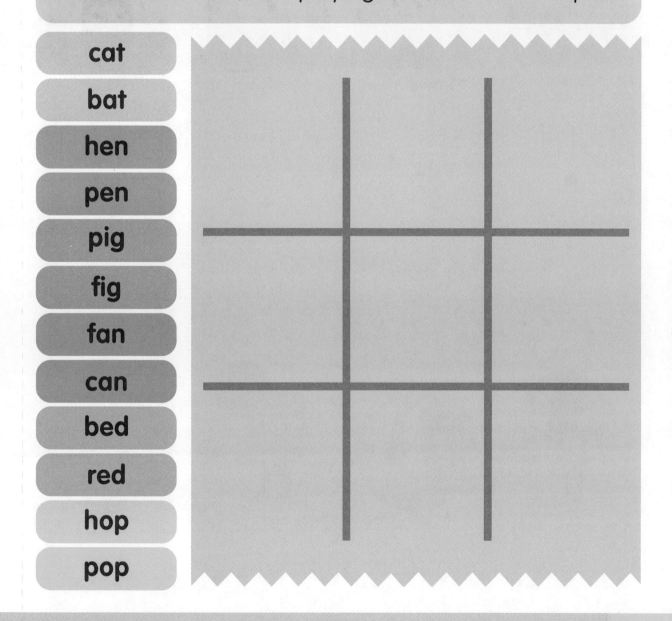

cat

bat

hen

pen

pig

fig

fan

can

bed

red

hop

pop

Match the Opposites

Trace each word, then **cover** it and **write** it on the line. Then match the word to its **opposite**.

old stop tall wet

old

dry short go new

Crossword Puzzle

Unscramble the letters to answer the clues.
Then write the answers in the **crossword puzzle**.
Use the pictures to help you.

Across

1 the opposite of big **s l m a l**
3 the opposite of under **v o r e**

Down

1 the opposite of fast **s l w o**
2 the opposite of hot **d l c o**

The Rainbow

Color it. **Spell** it. **Write** it.

red   r·e·d   ....

orange   o·r·a·n·g·e   ....

yellow   y·e·l·l·o·w   ....

green   g·r·e·e·n   ....

blue   b·l·u·e   ....

purple   p·u·r·p·l·e   ....

pink   p·i·n·k   ....

Finish the Picture

Finish the key by writing the **color** words. Then color the picture. Use the key and paint splashes to help you.

red

Capital Letters

Sentences start with capital letters.
Circle the letter that starts each sentence.

___ am happy.

I L t i J

___e went to the beach.

w M v W m

___he is my sister.

C c s B S

___o you like pizza?

D d b B P

People and Places

Names of **people** and **places** start with **capital letters**.
Trace the capital letters. Then rewrite the words
using capital letters in the right places.

Paris

Lily Coop
2 Oak Road
New Town

End the Sentence

Sentences end with **periods**, **question marks**, or **exclamation marks**. In each row, color the balloon with the correct punctuation mark.

I am
for telling.
•

I am
for yelling.
!

I am
for asking.
?

She rode her bike

Do you like cookies

Watch out

I am five years old

How are you

Surprise

Perfect Punctuation

Trace and write the **punctuation marks**.

Add a **punctuation mark** to each speech bubble.

Who are you

I am Luke

So am I

Doing Words

Doing words are called **verbs**. Say each sentence aloud. Then circle the child doing the correct action.

Simon says, "**Run!**"

Simon says, "**Jump!**"

Simon says, "**Read!**"

Simon says, "**Sing!**"

Describing Words

Describing words are called **adjectives**. Draw lines to match each sentence to the correct picture.

I am **tall**.

I am **cold**.

I am **soft** and **fluffy**.

I am **green** and **spiky**.

I am **pink** and **muddy**.

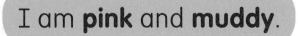

Sentence Scramble

Unscramble the words to make a **sentence** that matches the picture. Write the sentence.

| fed | I | fish. | my |

....

....

| picnic. | We | a | had |

....

....

| They | race. | ran | a |

....

....

Write Sentences

Write a **sentence** about each picture.

All About Me

Draw a picture of yourself. Then fill in the **speech bubbles** with facts about you.

My name is

....

I am ....
years old.

I like

....

My hair is

....

How to Dance

Write **instructions** for a dance using these moves.

spin around

jump up and down

wave your hands in the air

step from side to side

1 First, ...

2 Then, ...

3 After that, ...

4 Finally, ...

Ask someone to follow your **instructions**.
Do they get them right?

In My Opinion

Circle the ice-cream flavor **you like most**.
Then finish the sentences.

vanilla

chocolate

strawberry

mint
chocolate chip

cookies and
cream

My favorite flavor is ....

I like it because ....
....
....

Also, ...
....
....
....

Tell a Story

Look at the **pictures**, and make up a **story**. Draw what happens next in the last box. Then write your story.

The story's title is

....

One day, ...

....

After that, ...

....

....

In the end, ...

....

....

What's the Same?

Circle the picture that is the **same** as the first one.

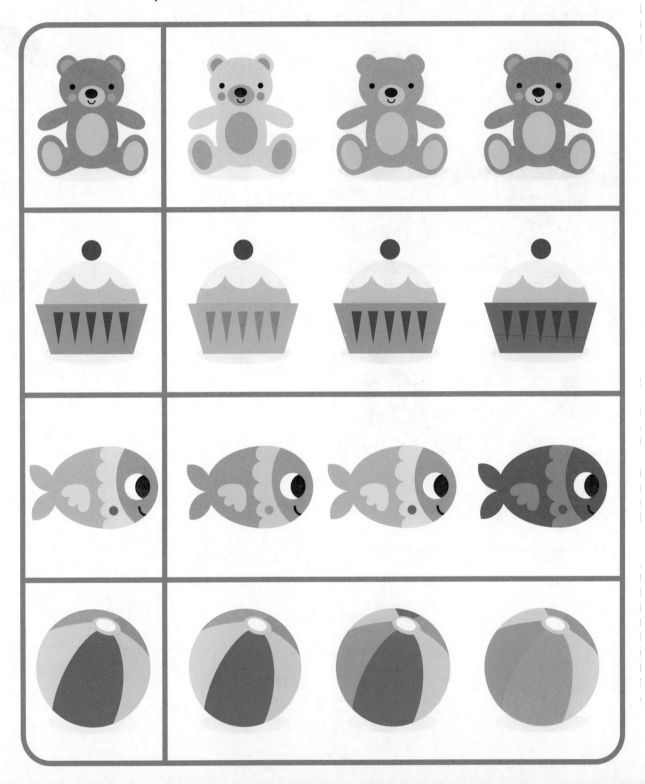

What's Different?

Circle the picture that is **different**.

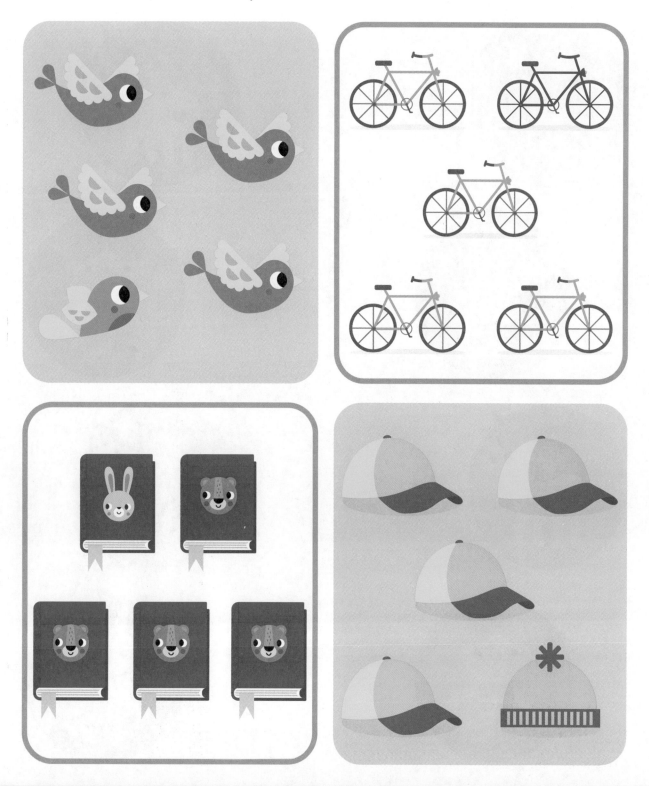

Match the Toys

Draw lines to match the toys that are the **same**.

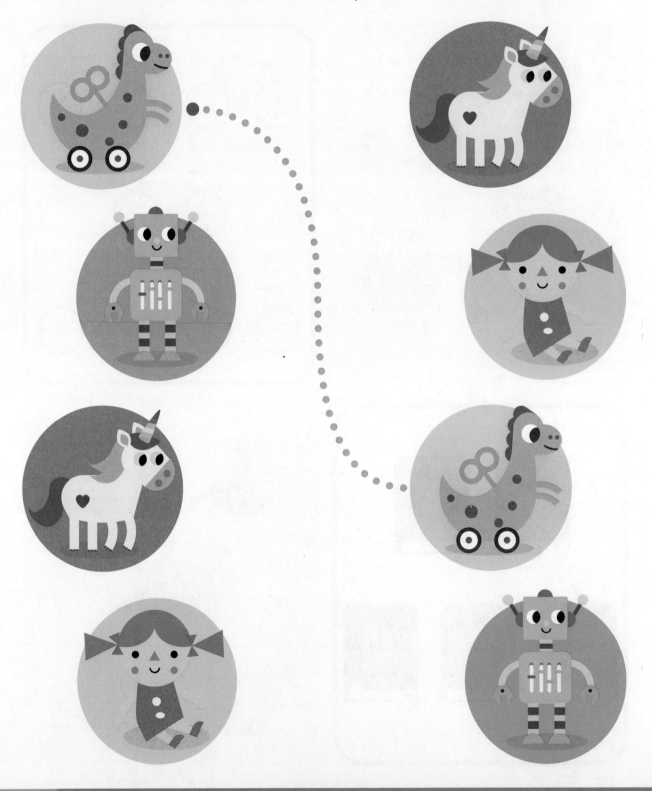

Match the Pets

Draw lines to match the pets of the **same type**.

Find the Differences

Find and circle **8** differences between the pictures.

Find the Differences

Find and circle **8** differences between the pictures.

Tidy Up Time

Draw lines to **sort** the craft materials into the jars.

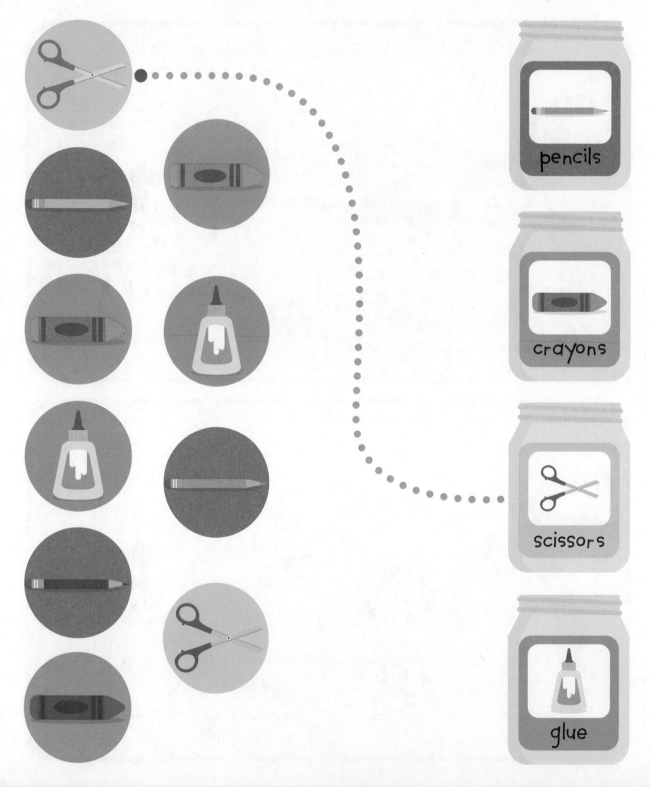

Find Our Place

Draw lines to **sort** the animals into groups.

We live in water.

We live on land.

We fly in the sky.

Group by Number

Circle the number that **matches** the **shopping list**.

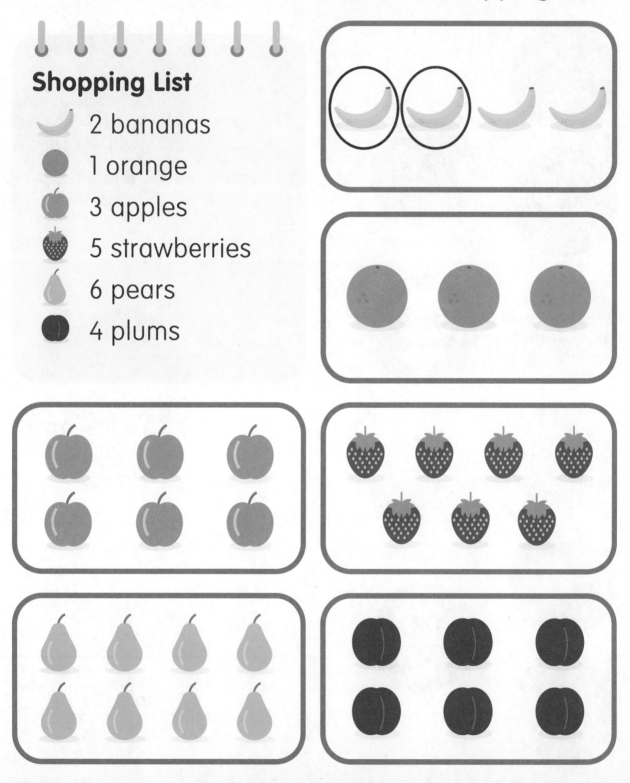

Shopping List

- 2 bananas
- 1 orange
- 3 apples
- 5 strawberries
- 6 pears
- 4 plums

Name the Groups

Circle the correct **group name**.

dogs   (fish)   birds

bikes   cars   boats

trees   cats   flowers

pizza   books   food

Sort the Animals

Draw lines to **sort** the animals **two** ways.

farm animals   wild animals

4 legs   2 legs

Sort the Clothes

Draw lines to **sort** the clothes **two** ways.

winter   summer

head   body

Sort the T-Shirts

Draw lines to **sort** the T-shirts **three** ways.

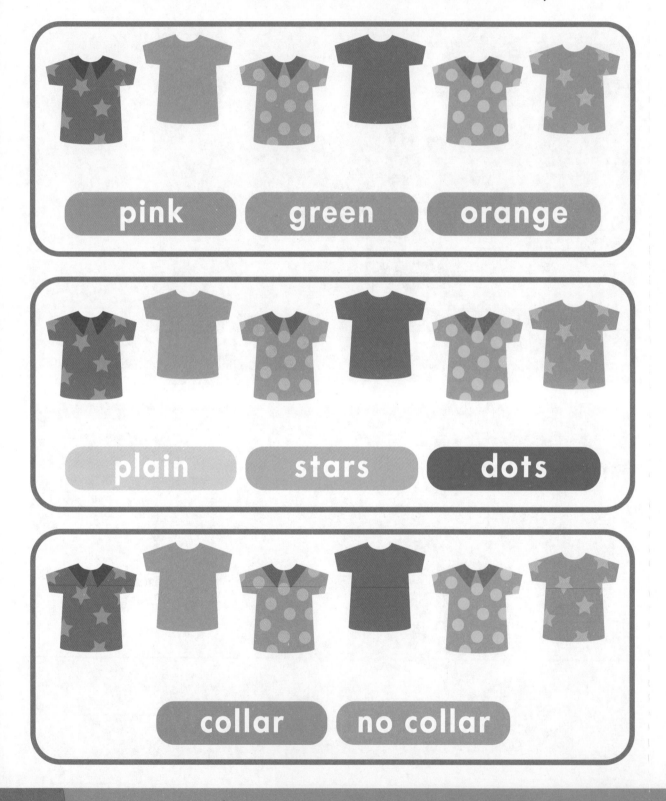

Sort the Monsters

Draw lines to **sort** the monsters **three** ways.

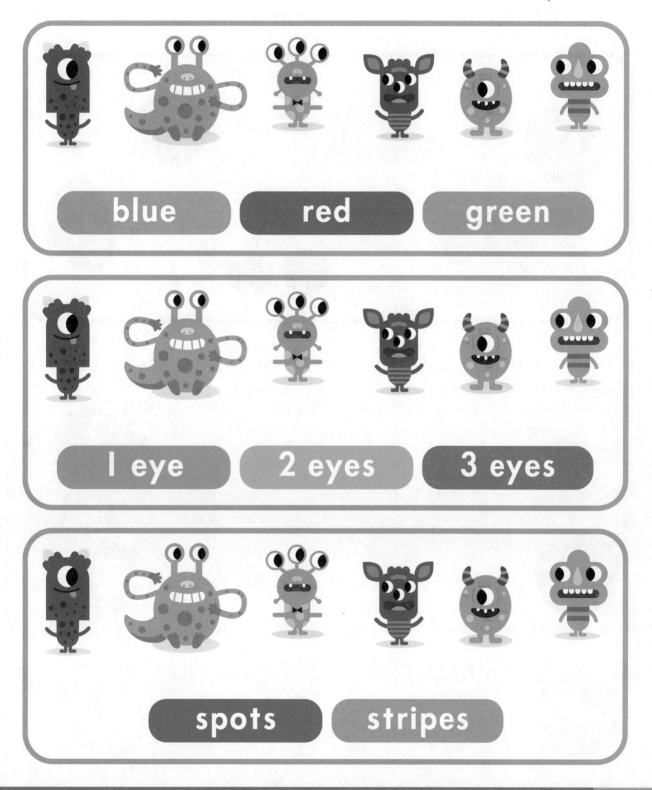

blue   red   green

l eye   2 eyes   3 eyes

spots   stripes

Sort the Fruit

Circle the **red** fruit with a **red** pencil.
Circle the **green** fruit with a **green** pencil.

Draw lines to match the fruits that are the **same color**.

Up and Down

Trace the words to label the arrows.

Color the things that are going **up** orange.
Color the things that are going **down** blue.

Left and Right

Trace the words under the hands.

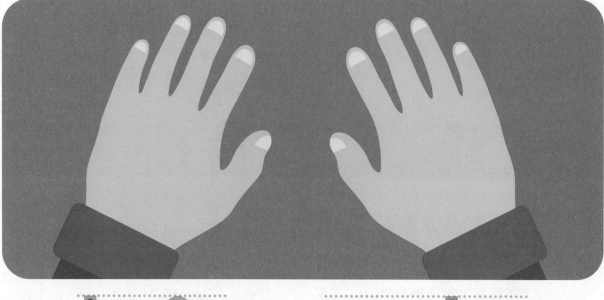

Circle the birds that are facing **left** in blue.
Circle the birds that are facing **right** in pink.

Find the Treasure

Follow the directions using the key
to draw a path to Pirate Pete's treasure.

Key: 🌴 = down, 🦜 = right, 🦀 = left, 🐵 = up

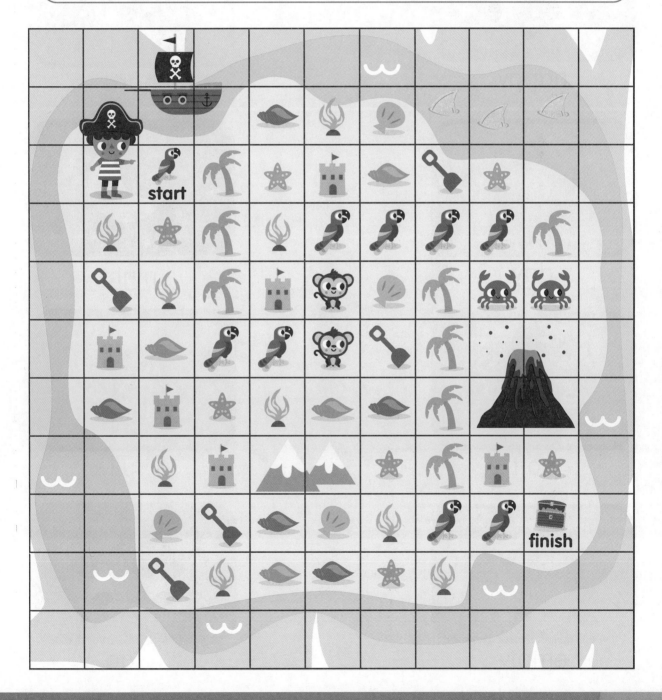

Opposites

Draw lines to match each picture to its **opposite**.

happy

hard

day

night

soft

full

empty

sad

Opposites

Draw lines to match each picture to its **opposite**.

dirty

shut

asleep

old

young

clean

open

awake

Count to 10

Trace the numbers. Then draw lines to **match** the numbers to the groups.

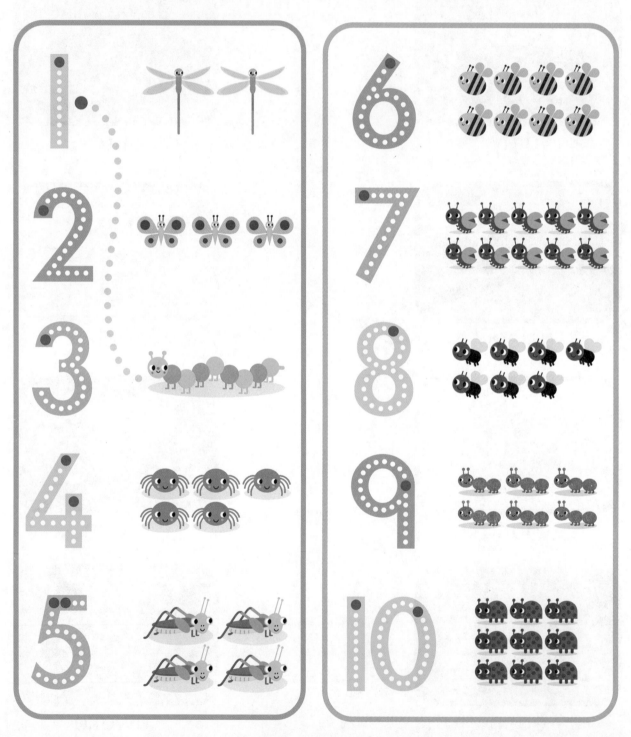

Count from 11 to 20

Count the balls in each group. **Write** the number, and **cross it out** in the number box.

11 ~~12~~ 13 14 15 16 17 18 19 20

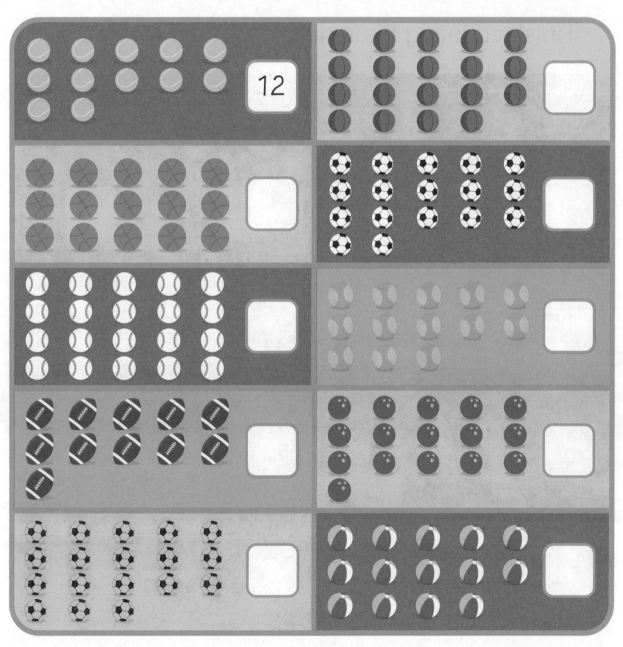

12

Count by 2's

Skip count by **2** to color every **second** box. Start at **2**.

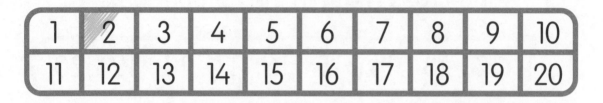

| 1 | 2 | 3 | 4 | 5 | 6 | 7 | 8 | 9 | 10 |
| 11 | 12 | 13 | 14 | 15 | 16 | 17 | 18 | 19 | 20 |

Finish counting the animals. Skip count by **2**'s.

Count by 5's

Skip count by **5** to color every **fifth** box. Start at **5**.

1	2	3	4	5	6	7	8	9	10
11	12	13	14	15	16	17	18	19	20
21	22	23	24	25	26	27	28	29	30
31	32	33	34	35	36	37	38	39	40
41	42	43	44	45	46	47	48	49	50

Finish counting the fingers. Skip count by **5**'s.

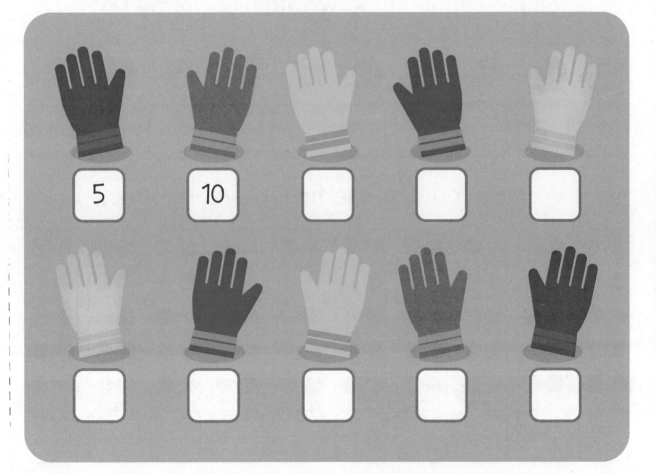

5   10

Count by 1's and 10's

Write the numbers in order from smallest to biggest.

8	4	9	2	5	10	1	7	3	6
1	2	__	__	__	__	__	__	__	__

40	10	70	60	90	100	30	20	80	50
10	20	__	__	__	__	__	__	__	__

Finish counting the **whales**. Count by **1**'s.

| 1 | 2 | | | | | | | | |

Finish counting the **fish**. Count by **10**'s.

| 10 | 20 | | | | | | | | |

Count by 10's

Skip count by **10** to color every **tenth** box. Start at **10**.

1	2	3	4	5	6	7	8	9	10
11	12	13	14	15	16	17	18	19	20
21	22	23	24	25	26	27	28	29	30
31	32	33	34	35	36	37	38	39	40
41	42	43	44	45	46	47	48	49	50
51	52	53	54	55	56	57	58	59	60
61	62	63	64	65	66	67	68	69	70
71	72	73	74	75	76	77	78	79	80
81	82	83	84	85	86	87	88	89	90
91	92	93	94	95	96	97	98	99	100

Finish counting the crayons. Skip count by **10**'s.

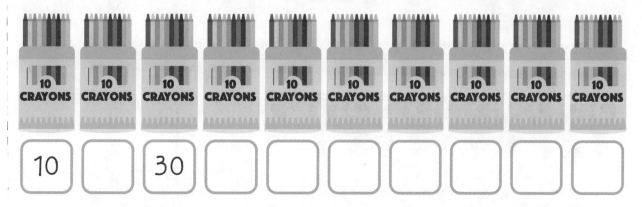

10		30							

189

10 and 1's

Count the objects by counting the **10** and then the **1's**.

tens	ones	number
1	2	12

tens	ones	number
___	___	___

tens	ones	number
___	___	___

tens	ones	number
___	___	___

tens	ones	number
___	___	___

10's and 1's

Count the objects by counting the **10**'s and then the **1**'s.

tens	ones	number
3	4	34

tens	ones	number

tens	ones	number

tens	ones	number

tens	ones	number

10's and 1's

Count the dots by counting the **10**'s and then the **1**'s.

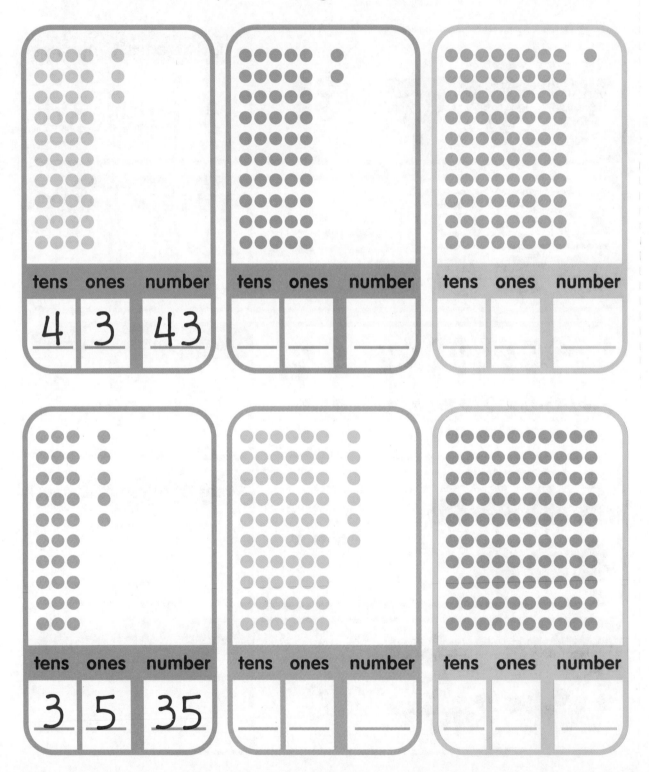

tens	ones	number
4	3	43

tens	ones	number

tens	ones	number

tens	ones	number
3	5	35

tens	ones	number

tens	ones	number

Number Patterns

Finish coloring the numbers that end with a 1 yellow.
Finish coloring the numbers that end with a **3 orange**.
Color the numbers that end with a **5 red**.
Color the numbers that end with a **7 purple**.
Color the numbers that end with a **9 blue**.

1	2	3	4	5	6	7	8	9	10
11	12	13	14	15	16	17	18	19	20
21	22	23	24	25	26	27	28	29	30
31	32	33	34	35	36	37	38	39	40
41	42	43	44	45	46	47	48	49	50
51	52	53	54	55	56	57	58	59	60
61	62	63	64	65	66	67	68	69	70
71	72	73	74	75	76	77	78	79	80
81	82	83	84	85	86	87	88	89	90
91	92	93	94	95	96	97	98	99	100

Count the Beetles

Circle **groups of 10** beetles. Then count how many are left over. Add the **10**'s and **1**'s to count the beetles.

There are ☐ beetles.

Bigger or Smaller

Count the **10**'s and the **1**'s. Then circle the biggest group of dots in each pair.

Write > (**bigger than**) or < (**smaller than**) between each number pair.

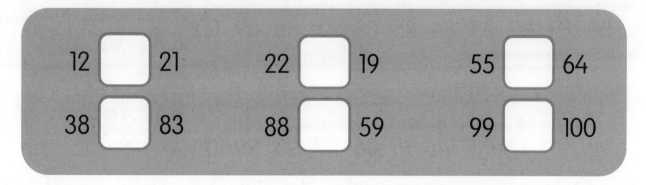

| 12 | | 21 | | 22 | | 19 | | 55 | | 64 |
| 38 | | 83 | | 88 | | 59 | | 99 | | 100 |

Number Lines

Draw an arrow on the **number line** to show the problem.
Then write the answer.

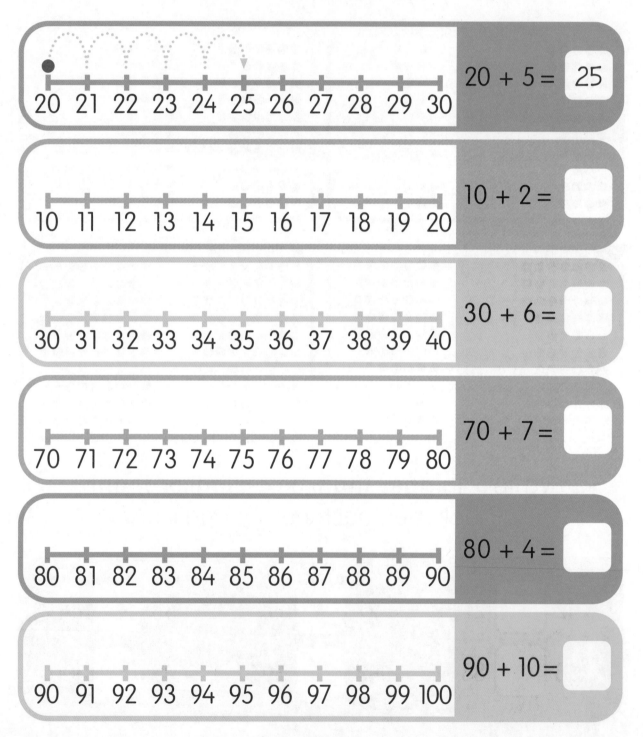

20 + 5 = **25**

10 + 2 =

30 + 6 =

70 + 7 =

80 + 4 =

90 + 10 =

Count Forward

Count forward from the starting number to fill the cars.

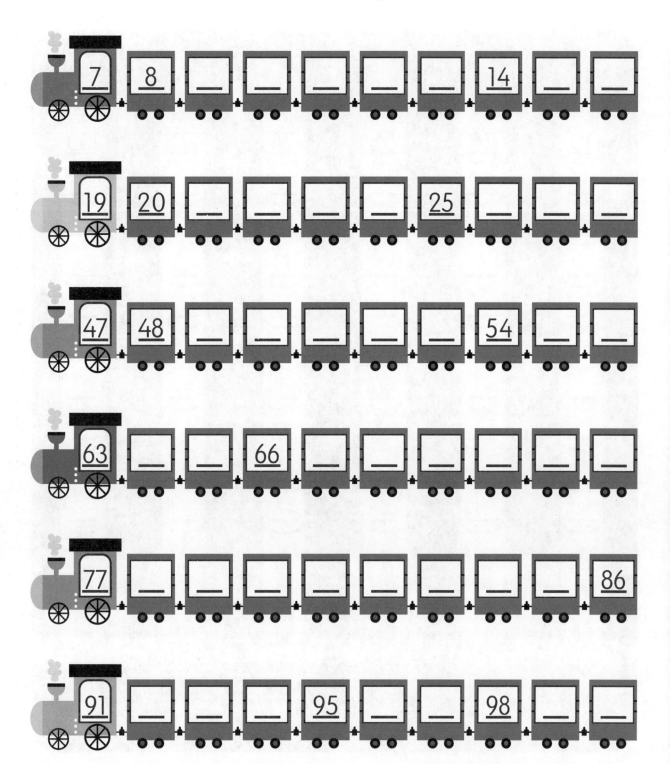

7 | 8 | | | | | | 14 | |

19 | 20 | | | | | 25 | | |

47 | 48 | | | | | 54 | |

63 | | | 66 | | | | | |

77 | | | | | | | | 86

91 | | | 95 | | 98 | |

Count Down

Count down from the starting number to fill the rockets.

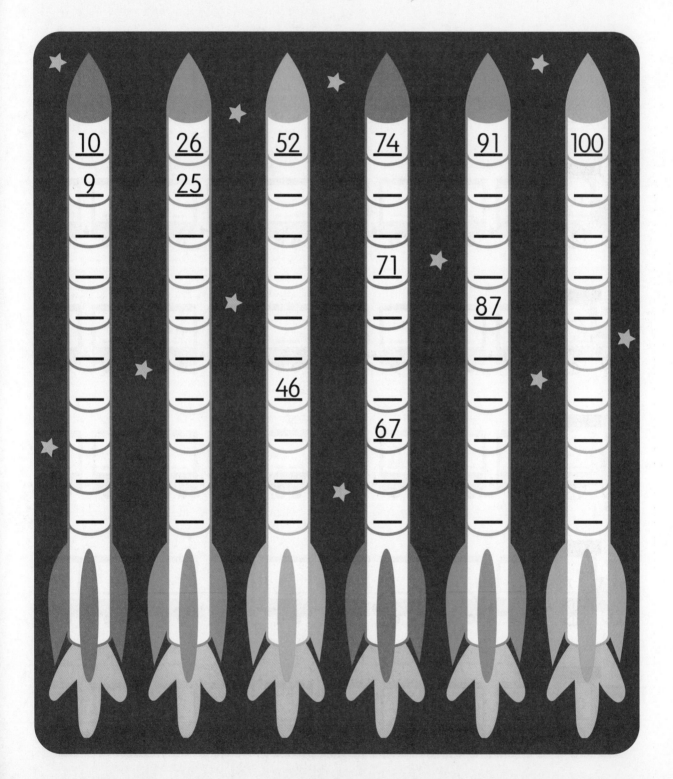

10	26	52	74	91	100
9	25	—	—	—	—
—	—	—	71	87	—
—	—	46	—	—	—
—	—	—	67	—	—
—	—	—	—	—	—
—	—	—	—	—	—

Order Numbers

In each group, color the **biggest** number **purple**, the **middle** number yellow, and the **smallest** number green.

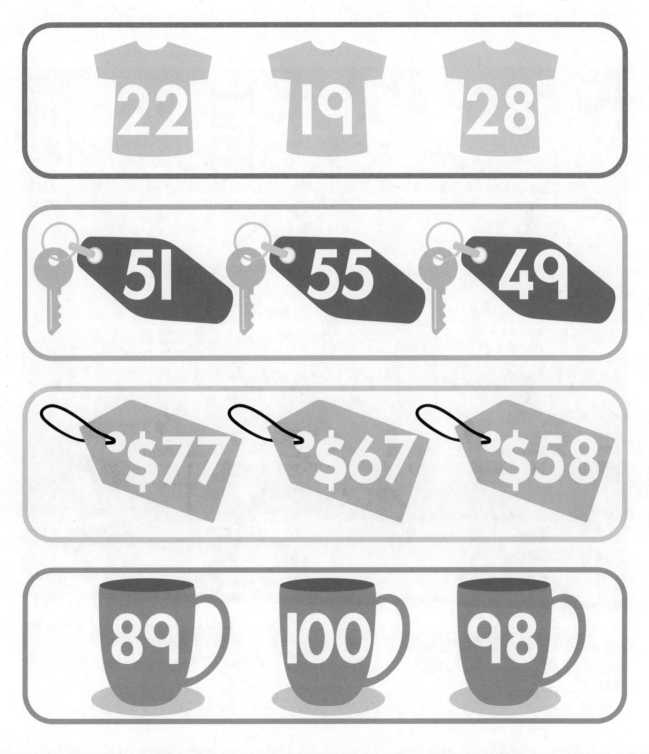

Snakes and Ladders

Find a partner, two counters, and a dice.
Start at **1**. If you land on a **ladder**, climb it. If you land on a **snake**, slide down it. The first person to **100** wins!

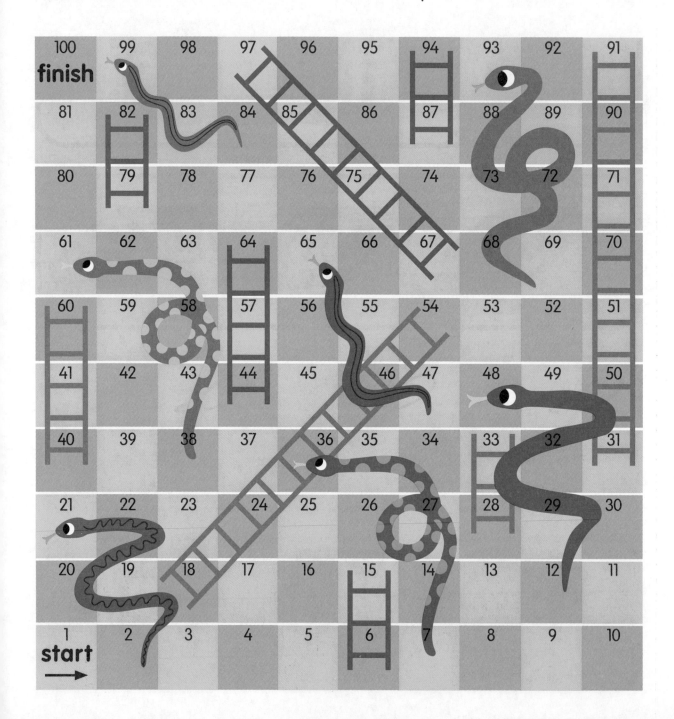

Count to 100!

Fill in the missing numbers on the hundred chart to show that you can count to **100**.

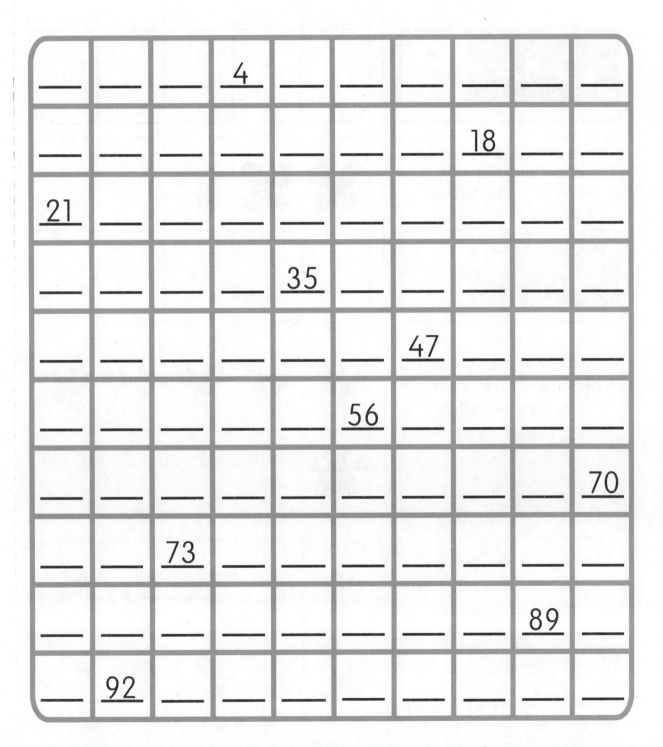

Use Ten Frames

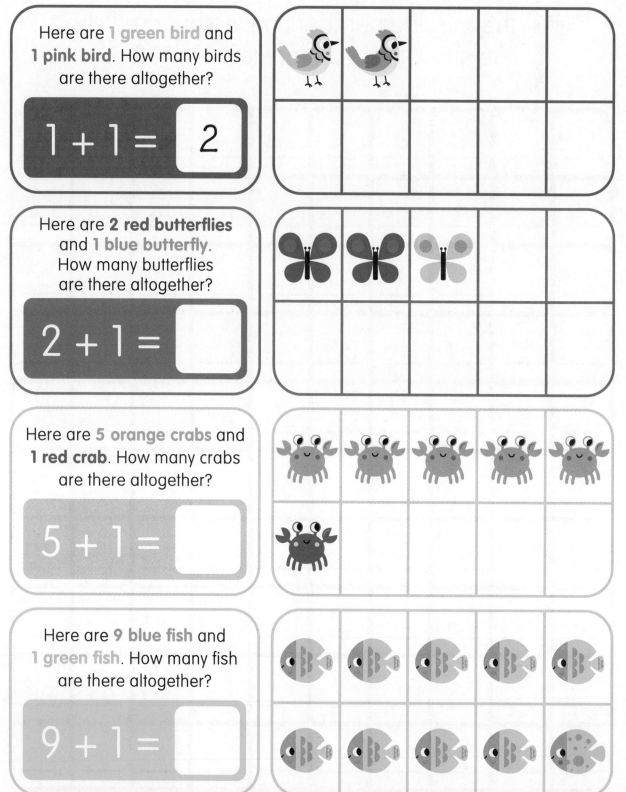

Here are **1 green bird** and **1 pink bird**. How many birds are there altogether?

1 + 1 = **2**

Here are **2 red butterflies** and **1 blue butterfly**. How many butterflies are there altogether?

2 + 1 =

Here are **5 orange crabs** and **1 red crab**. How many crabs are there altogether?

5 + 1 =

Here are **9 blue fish** and **1 green fish**. How many fish are there altogether?

9 + 1 =

Use Ten Frames

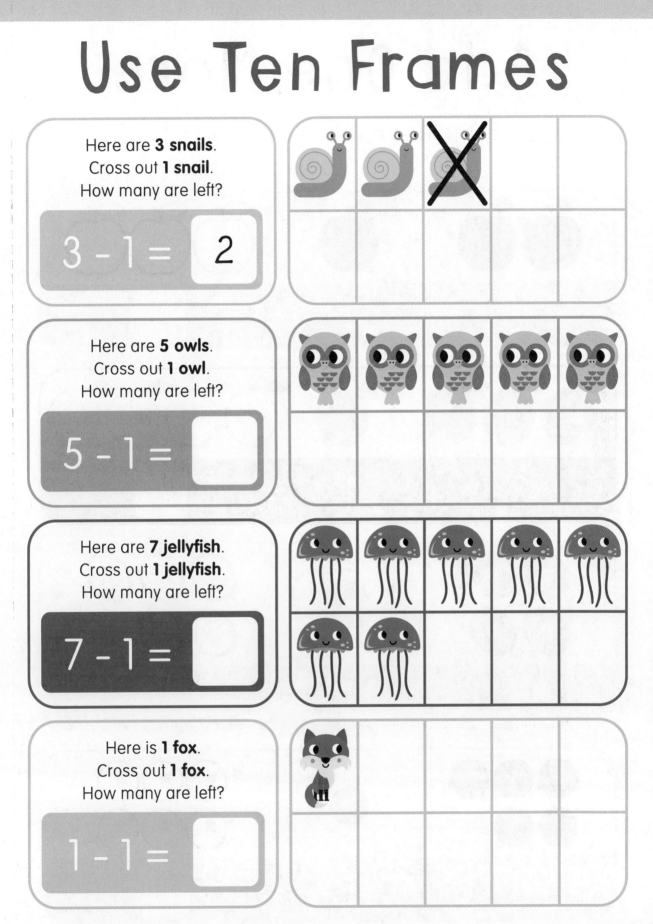

Here are **3 snails**.
Cross out **1 snail**.
How many are left?

3 - 1 = 2

Here are **5 owls**.
Cross out **1 owl**.
How many are left?

5 - 1 =

Here are **7 jellyfish**.
Cross out **1 jellyfish**.
How many are left?

7 - 1 =

Here is **1 fox**.
Cross out **1 fox**.
How many are left?

1 - 1 =

Add One More

Add **1** to the first number and color the fruits
to solve the problems.

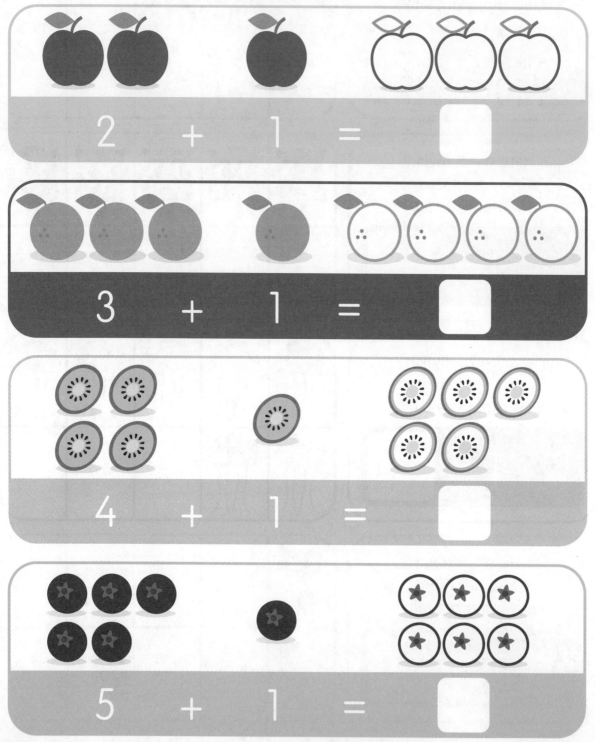

2 + 1 =

3 + 1 =

4 + 1 =

5 + 1 =

Subtract One

Cross out **1** from each row to help
solve the problems.

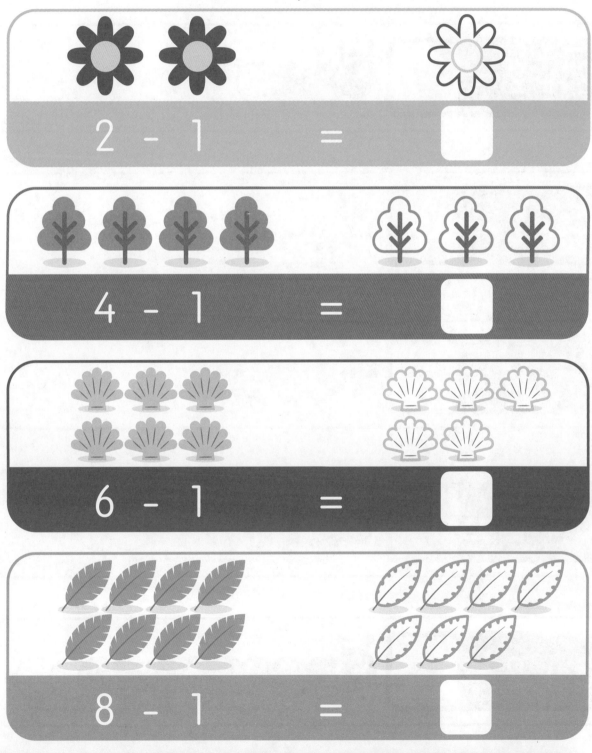

2 - 1 =

4 - 1 =

6 - 1 =

8 - 1 =

Add Two More

Add **2** to the first number and finish coloring the caterpillars to solve the problems.

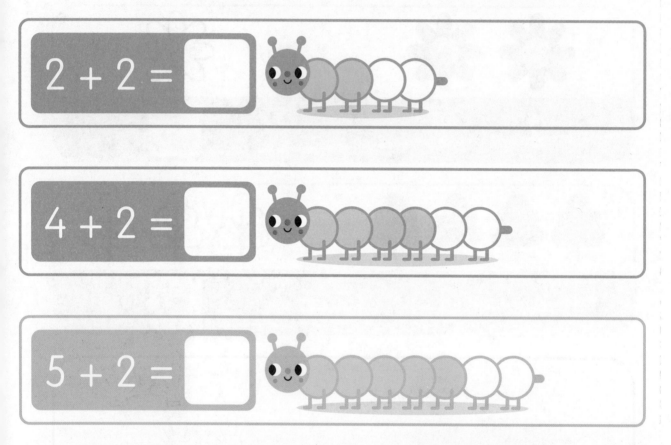

2 + 2 =

4 + 2 =

5 + 2 =

6 + 2 =

8 + 2 =

Subtract Two

Cross out **2** from each row to help solve the problems.

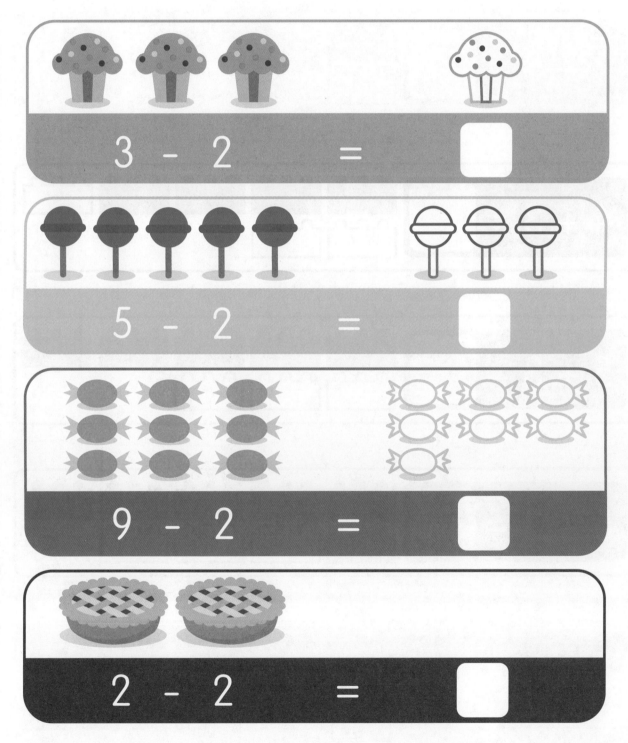

3 - 2 =

5 - 2 =

9 - 2 =

2 - 2 =

Add Three More

Add **3** to the first number and finish coloring
the blocks to solve the problems.

$3 + 3 = \boxed{}$

$4 + 3 = \boxed{}$

$5 + 3 = \boxed{}$

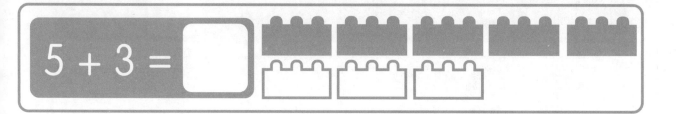

$6 + 3 = \boxed{}$

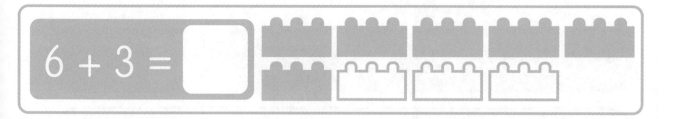

$7 + 3 = \boxed{}$

Subtract Three

Cross out **3** from each row to help solve the problems.

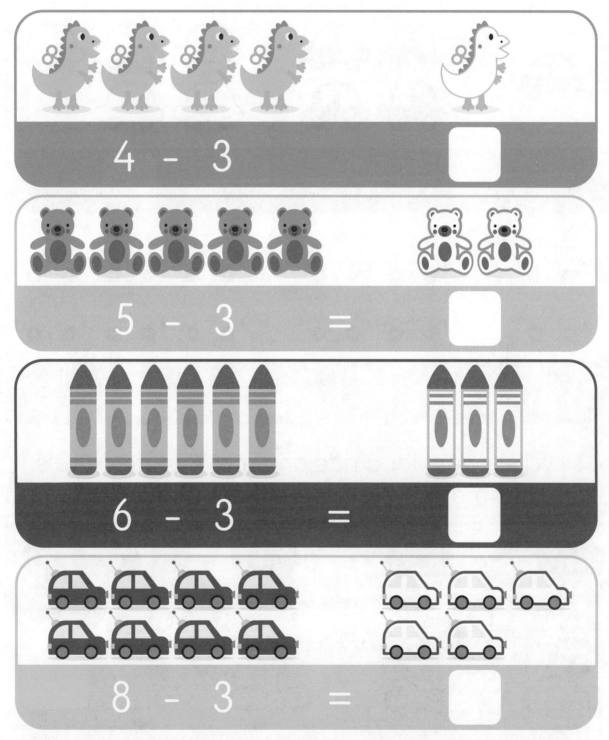

4 - 3

5 - 3 =

6 - 3 =

8 - 3 =

Add Four More

Add **4** to the first number and finish coloring
the cars to solve the problems.

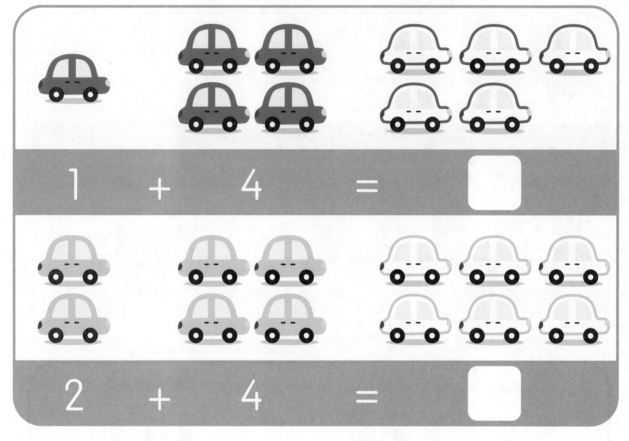

$$1 + 4 = \boxed{}$$

$$2 + 4 = \boxed{}$$

3 cyclists went for a ride and met **4** more cyclists.
How many cyclists were there altogether?

Subtract Four

Cross out **4** from each box to help solve the problems.

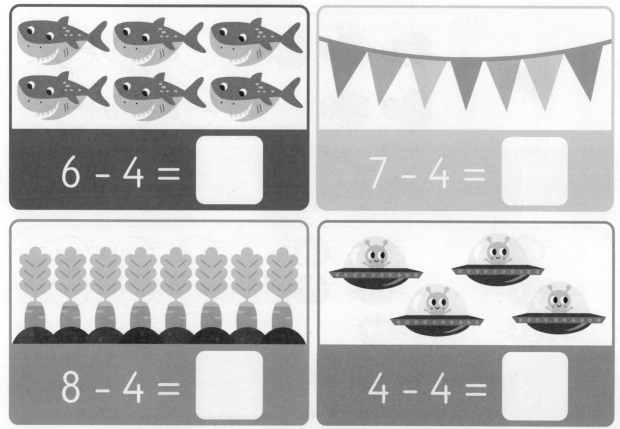

6 - 4 =

7 - 4 =

8 - 4 =

4 - 4 =

Lily had **9** candies in a jar. She took out **4**. How many candies were left?

Add Five More

Add **5** to the first number and finish coloring
the bugs to solve the problems.

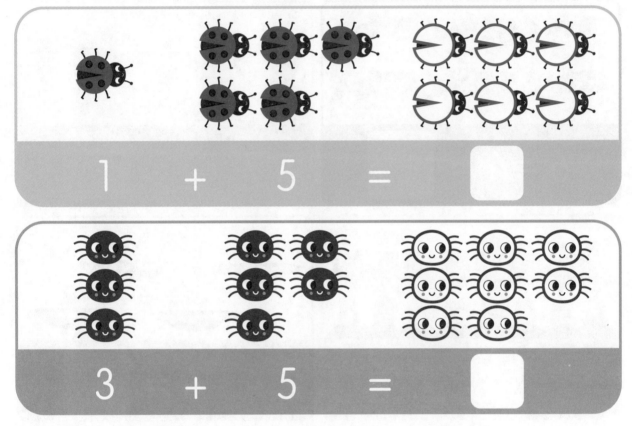

1 + 5 = ☐

3 + 5 = ☐

5 monkeys met **5** more monkeys.
How many monkeys were there altogether?

Subtract Five

Cross out **5** from each box to help
solve the problems.

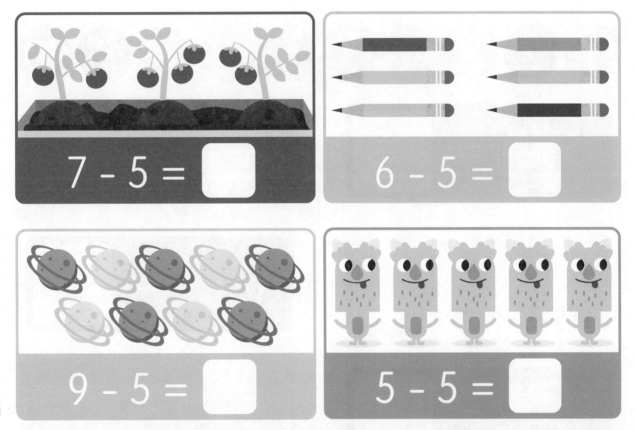

7 - 5 =

6 - 5 =

9 - 5 =

5 - 5 =

Eddie made **12** cupcakes. He gave **5** to his friends.
How many cupcakes were left?

Practice Adding

Solve the problems. Use the numbers at the top of the page if you need to.

1 2 3 4 5 6 7 8 9 10

$5 + 4 =$

$3 + 5 =$

$4 + 3 =$

$6 + 4 =$

$7 + 2 =$

$5 + 2 =$

$2 + 6 =$

$3 + 6 =$

$8 + 2 =$

$7 + 3 =$

Practice Subtracting

Solve the problems. Use the numbers at the top of the page if you need to.

1 2 3 4 5 6 7 8 9 10

8 - 6 = [ ]

9 - 7 = [ ]

6 - 3 = [ ]

7 - 4 = [ ]

9 - 5 = [ ]

5 - 3 = [ ]

5 - 4 = [ ]

8 - 5 = [ ]

7 - 3 = [ ]

6 - 4 = [ ]

Add Ten More

Add **10** to the first number and finish coloring the balloons to solve the problems.

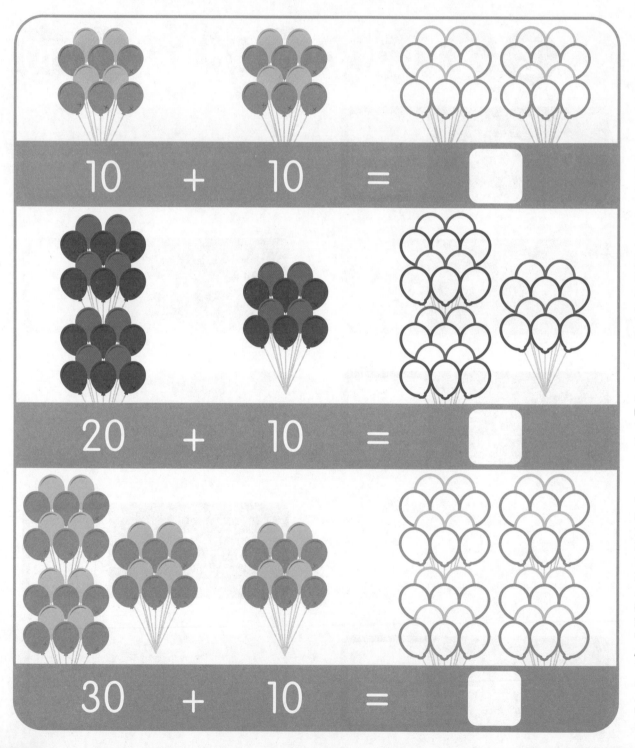

10 + 10 =

20 + 10 =

30 + 10 =

Subtract Ten

Cross out **10** from each box to help
solve the problems.

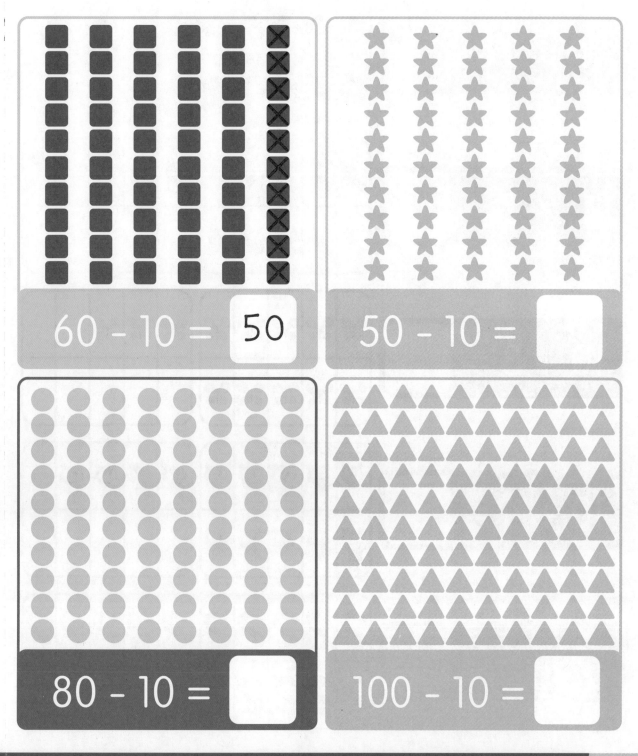

60 − 10 = 50

50 − 10 =

80 − 10 =

100 − 10 =

Add on to 10

Use the ten frames to solve the problems.

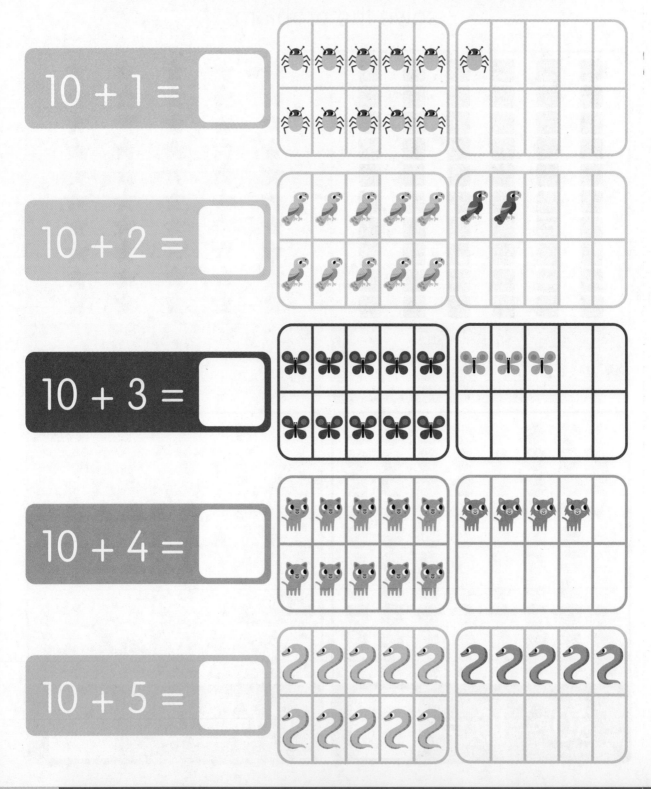

10 + 1 =

10 + 2 =

10 + 3 =

10 + 4 =

10 + 5 =

Add on to 10

Use the ten frames to solve the problems.

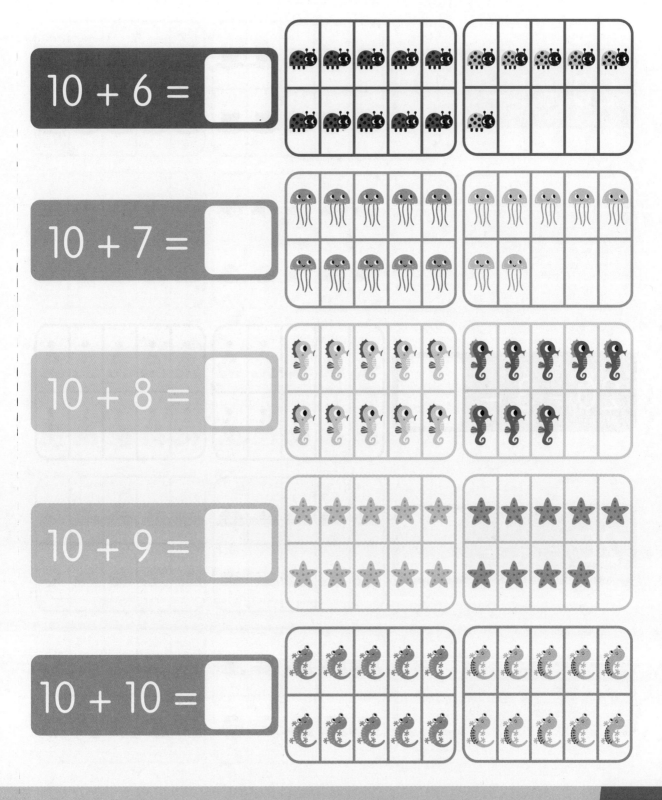

10 + 6 =

10 + 7 =

10 + 8 =

10 + 9 =

10 + 10 =

Subtract from 20

Cross out hats to help solve the problems.

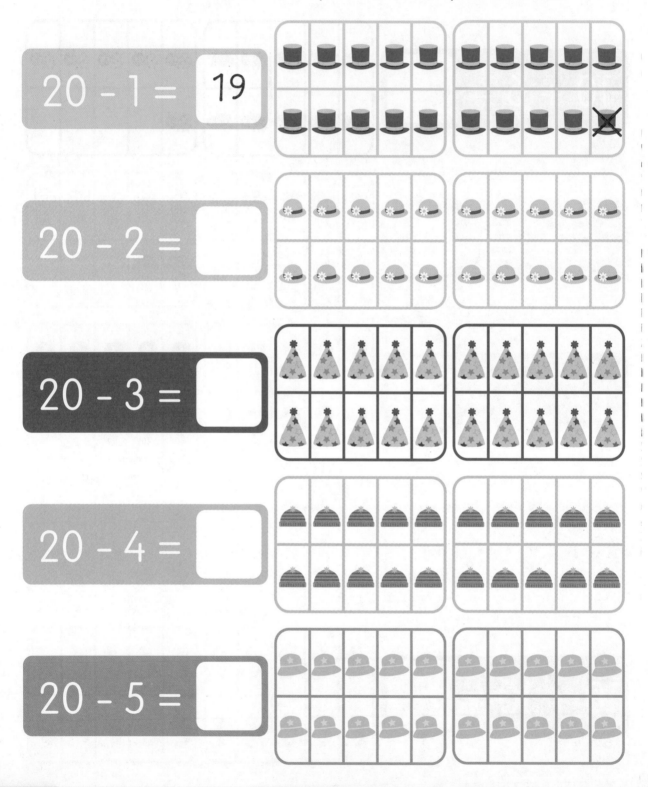

20 − 1 = **19**

20 − 2 =

20 − 3 =

20 − 4 =

20 − 5 =

Subtract from 20

Cross out socks to help solve the problems.

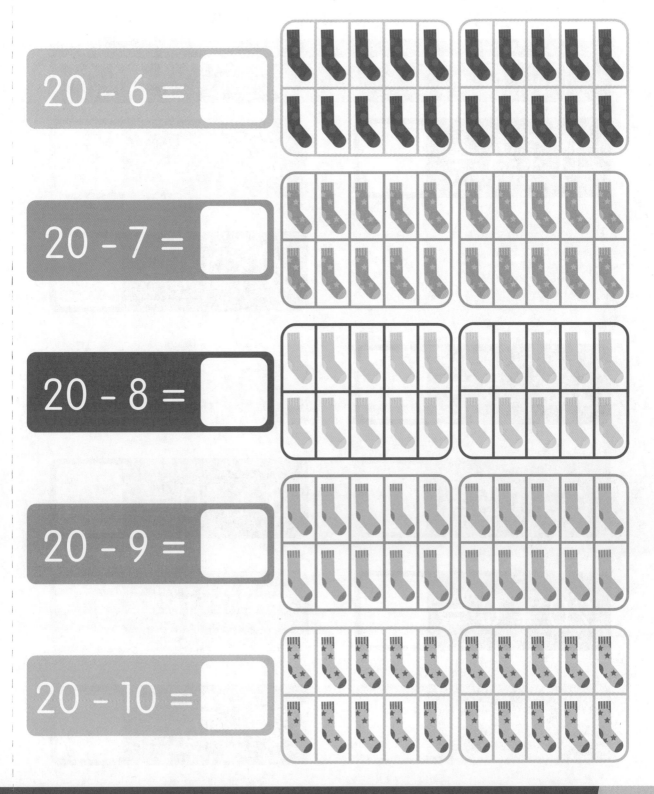

20 - 6 =

20 - 7 =

20 - 8 =

20 - 9 =

20 - 10 =

Practice Adding

Solve the problems.
Use the number line if you need to.

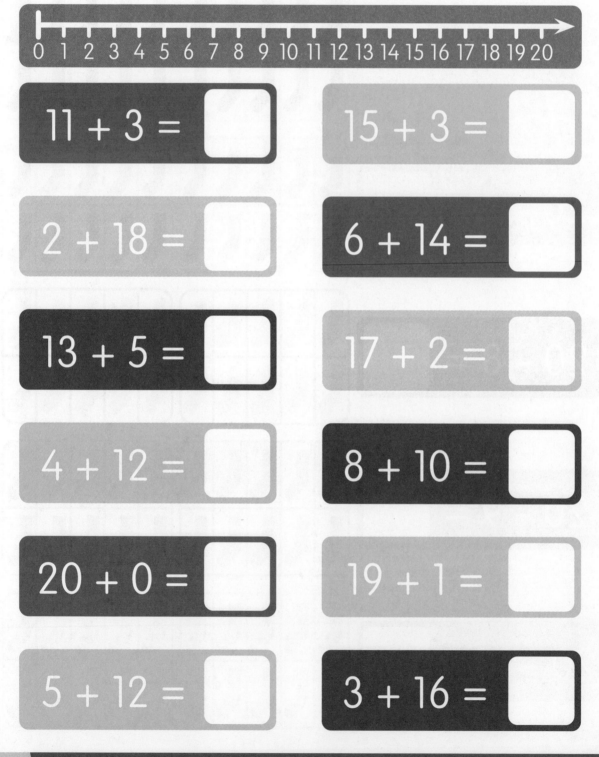

0 1 2 3 4 5 6 7 8 9 10 11 12 13 14 15 16 17 18 19 20

11 + 3 = ☐

15 + 3 = ☐

2 + 18 = ☐

6 + 14 = ☐

13 + 5 = ☐

17 + 2 = ☐

4 + 12 = ☐

8 + 10 = ☐

20 + 0 = ☐

19 + 1 = ☐

5 + 12 = ☐

3 + 16 = ☐

Practice Adding

Fill in the missing numbers.
Use the number line if you need to.

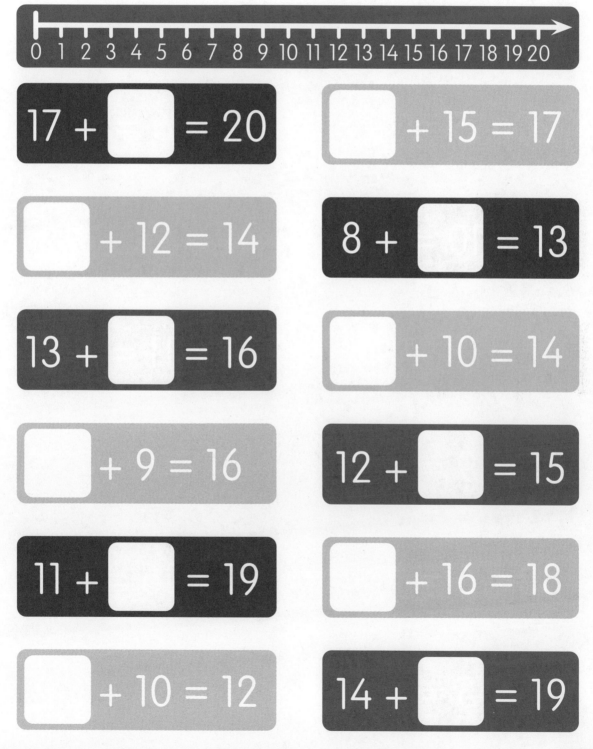

$$17 + \boxed{} = 20$$

$$\boxed{} + 15 = 17$$

$$\boxed{} + 12 = 14$$

$$8 + \boxed{} = 13$$

$$13 + \boxed{} = 16$$

$$\boxed{} + 10 = 14$$

$$\boxed{} + 9 = 16$$

$$12 + \boxed{} = 15$$

$$11 + \boxed{} = 19$$

$$\boxed{} + 16 = 18$$

$$\boxed{} + 10 = 12$$

$$14 + \boxed{} = 19$$

Practice Subtracting

Solve the problems.
Use the number line if you need to.

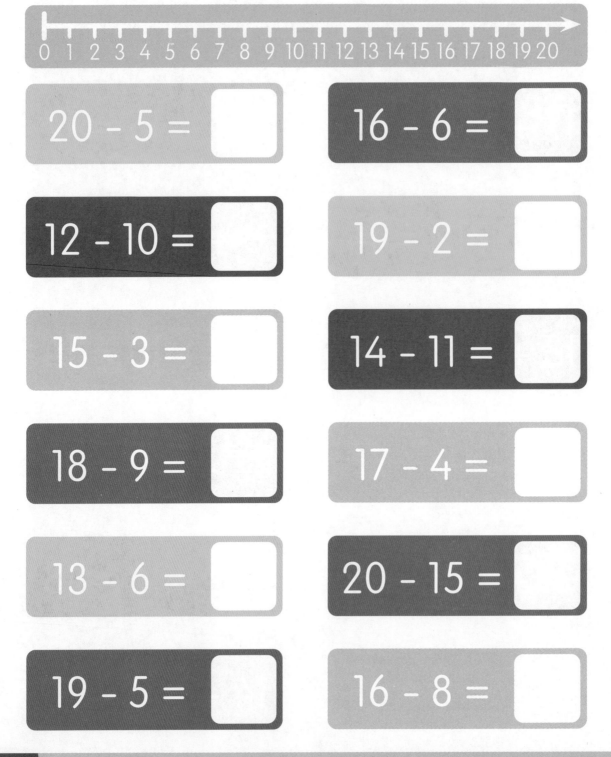

0 1 2 3 4 5 6 7 8 9 10 11 12 13 14 15 16 17 18 19 20

20 – 5 = ☐

16 – 6 = ☐

12 – 10 = ☐

19 – 2 = ☐

15 – 3 = ☐

14 – 11 = ☐

18 – 9 = ☐

17 – 4 = ☐

13 – 6 = ☐

20 – 15 = ☐

19 – 5 = ☐

16 – 8 = ☐

Practice Subtracting

Fill in the missing numbers.
Use the number line if you need to.

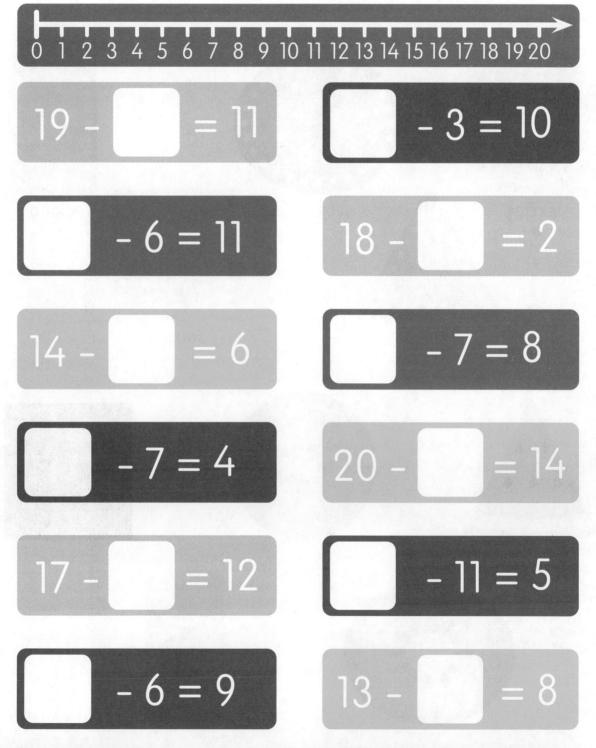

0 1 2 3 4 5 6 7 8 9 10 11 12 13 14 15 16 17 18 19 20

$19 - \boxed{} = 11$

$\boxed{} - 3 = 10$

$\boxed{} - 6 = 11$

$18 - \boxed{} = 2$

$14 - \boxed{} = 6$

$\boxed{} - 7 = 8$

$\boxed{} - 7 = 4$

$20 - \boxed{} = 14$

$17 - \boxed{} = 12$

$\boxed{} - 11 = 5$

$\boxed{} - 6 = 9$

$13 - \boxed{} = 8$

Match the 2D Shapes

Trace the **2D shapes**. Then draw lines
to match the **shapes** to the **objects**.

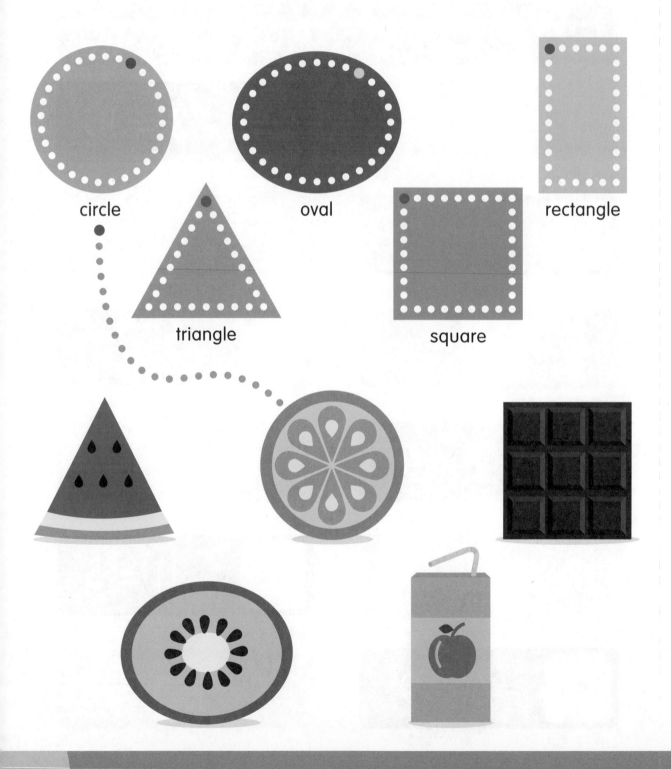

circle

oval

rectangle

triangle

square

Count the Sides

Count the **sides** on each shape.
Then match the **shape** to the **number**.

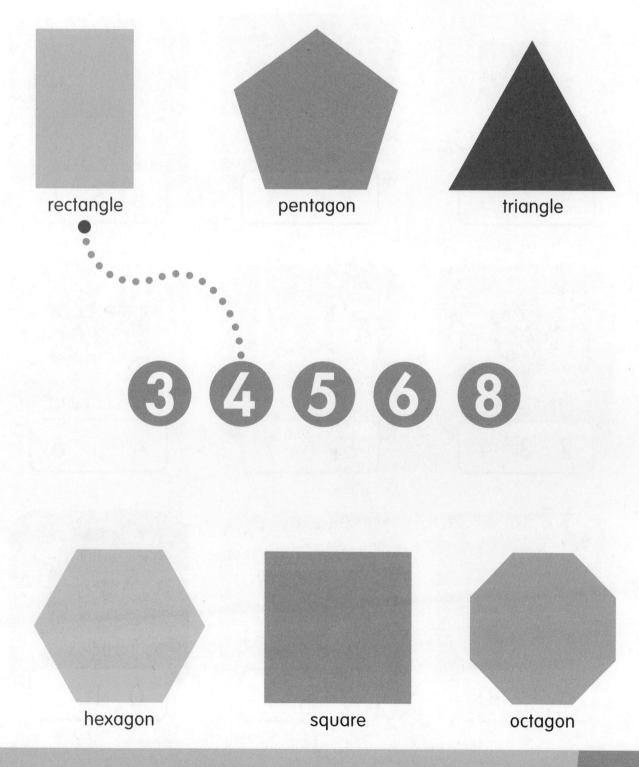

rectangle

pentagon

triangle

3 4 5 6 8

hexagon

square

octagon

227

Count the Corners

Count the **corners** on each shape.
Then circle the correct **number**.

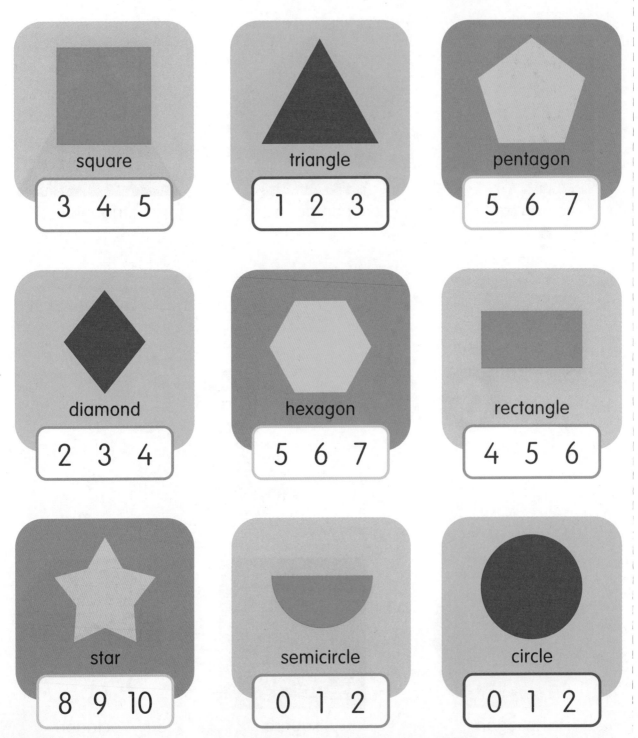

square
3 4 5

triangle
1 2 3

pentagon
5 6 7

diamond
2 3 4

hexagon
5 6 7

rectangle
4 5 6

star
8 9 10

semicircle
0 1 2

circle
0 1 2

Shape Art

Use the **key** to finish **coloring** the shape art.

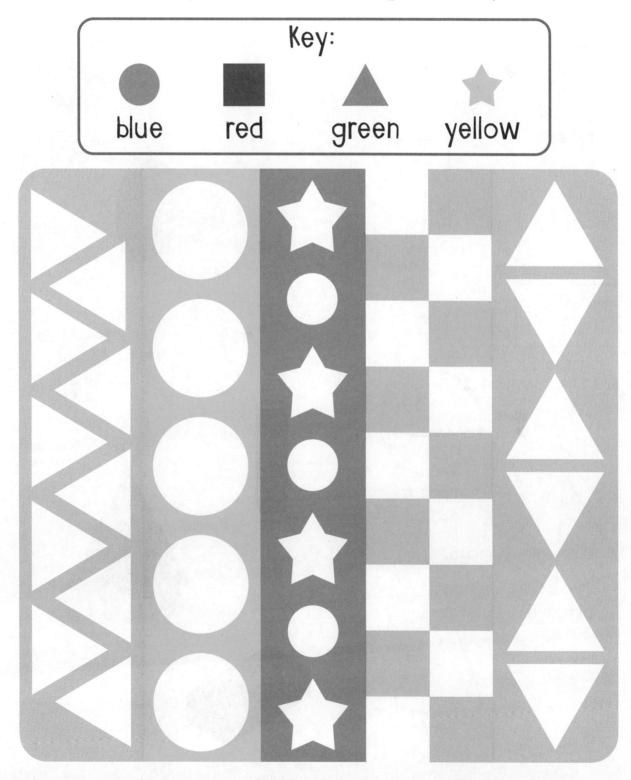

Match the 3D Shapes

Match the **3D shapes** to the **objects**.

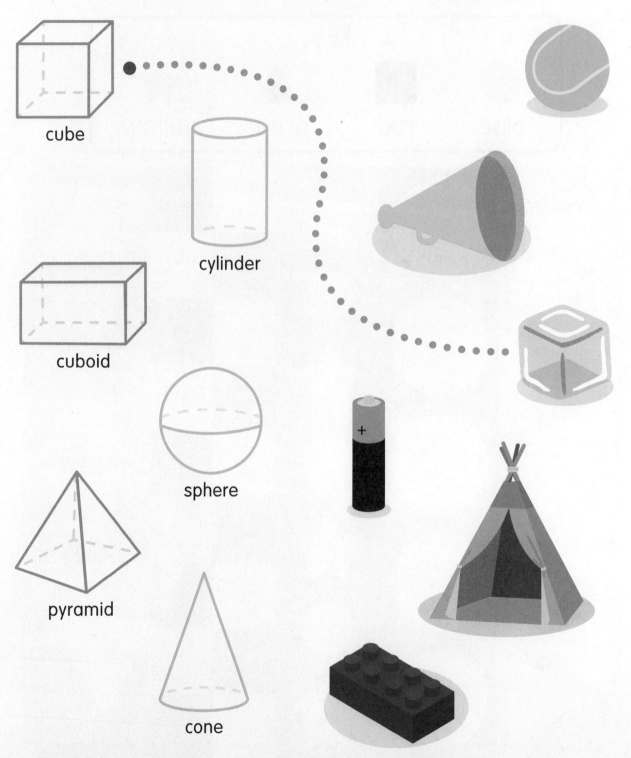

cube

cylinder

cuboid

sphere

pyramid

cone

3D Blocks

Use the **key** to **color** the block castle.

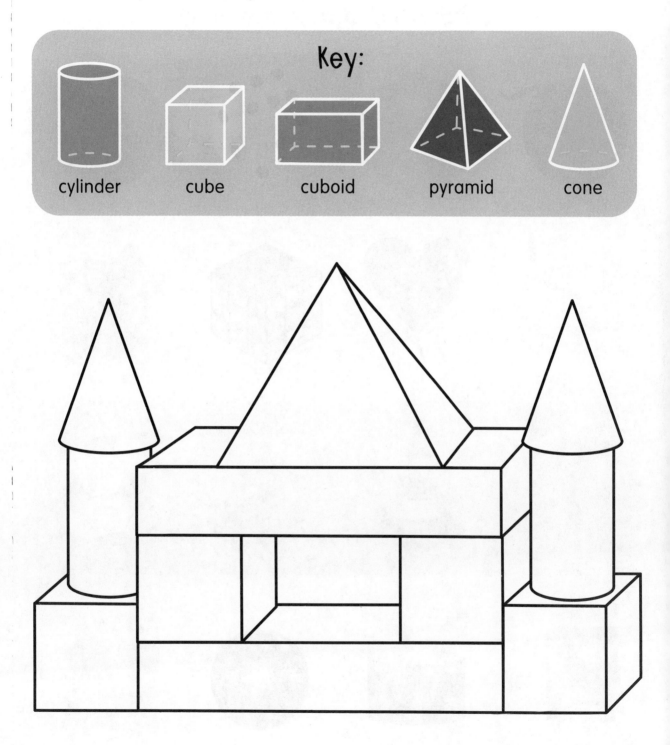

Key:

cylinder   cube   cuboid   pyramid   cone

A World of Shapes

Circle the **3D object** in each row that is
a **different shape** to the others.

Make a Pyramid

You will need:

crayons

clear tape

safety scissors

Instructions:

1 Color the pyramid net above.

2 Carefully pull out this page, and cut along the thick green lines around the pyramid net.

3 Fold the shape along the dashed lines to make a pyramid.

4 Tape the sides in place.

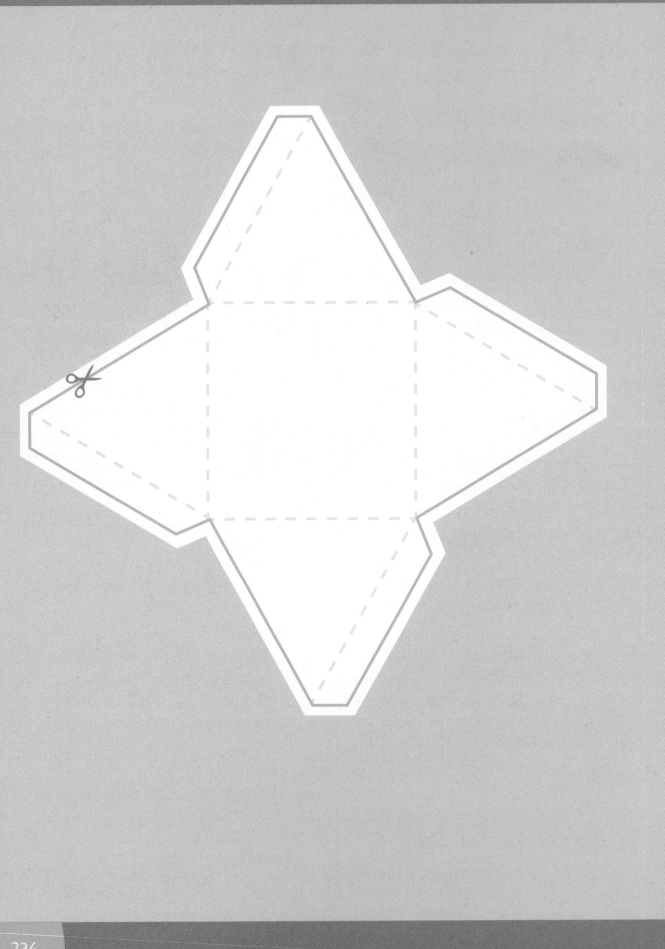

Shape Symmetry

When the two halves of an object are mirror images, they are **symmetrical**. Color the other **half** of each picture in the **same colors** to make it **symmetrical**.

Long or Short

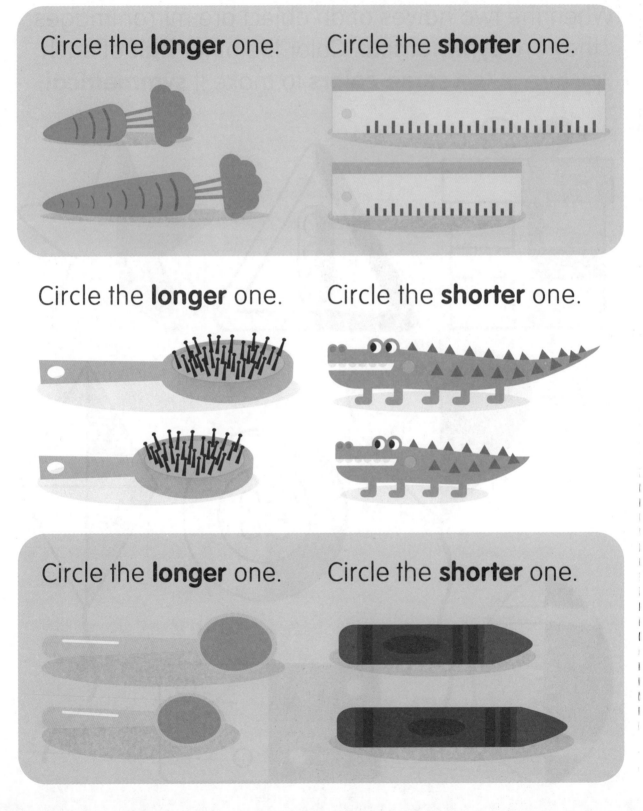

Circle the **longer** one.

Circle the **shorter** one.

Circle the **longer** one.

Circle the **shorter** one.

Circle the **longer** one.

Circle the **shorter** one.

Tall or Short

Circle the **shorter** one. Circle the **taller** one.

Circle the **shorter** one. Circle the **taller** one.

Circle the **shorter** one. Circle the **taller** one.

Wide or Narrow

Color the **wide** gate **red** and the **narrow** gate **blue**.

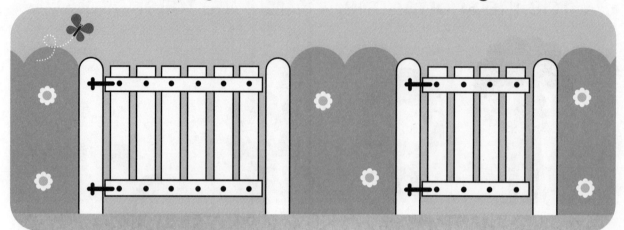

Color the **wide** bed **orange** and the **narrow** bed **purple**.

Color the **narrow** boat **yellow** and the **wide** boat **green**.

More or Less

Circle the picture in each pair that shows **more**.

More or Fewer

Circle the picture in each pair that shows **fewer**.

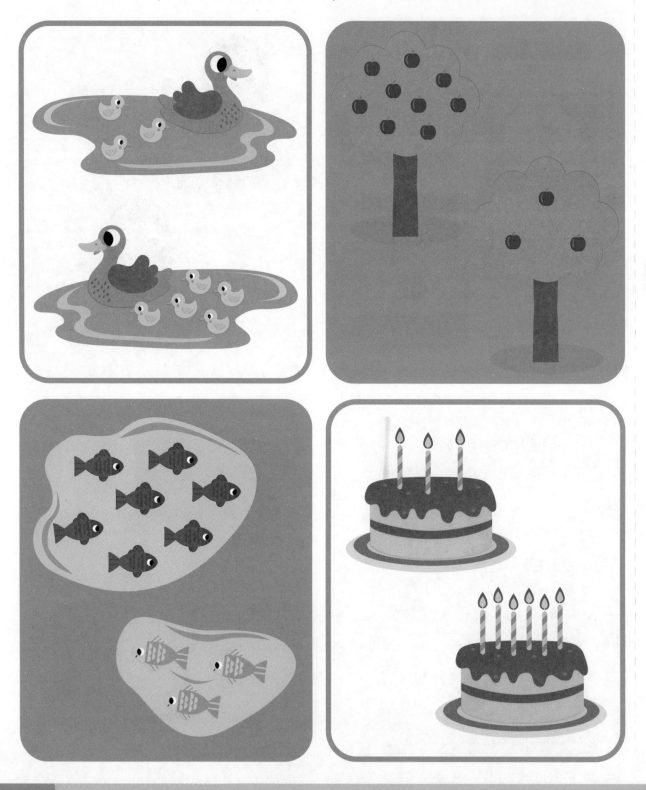

Empty to Full

Write **1** by the containers that are **empty**.
Write **2** by the containers that are **half full**.
Write **3** by the containers that are **full**.

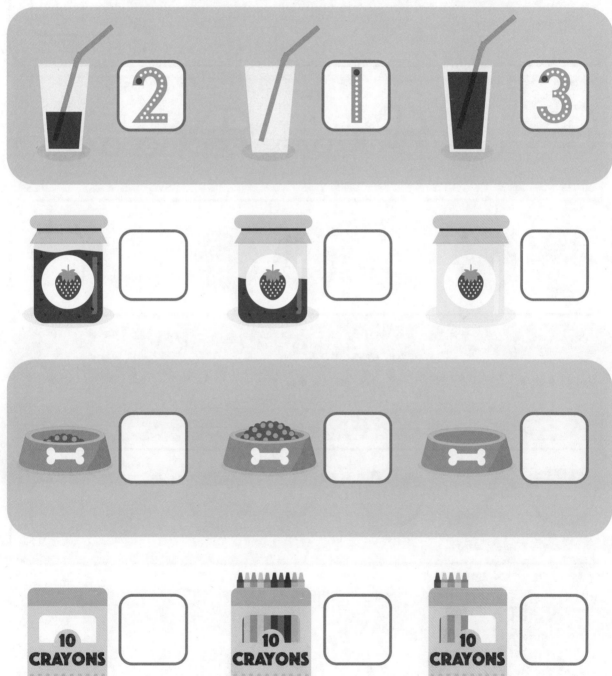

Find the Pattern

How many **different pictures** make up each **pattern**?

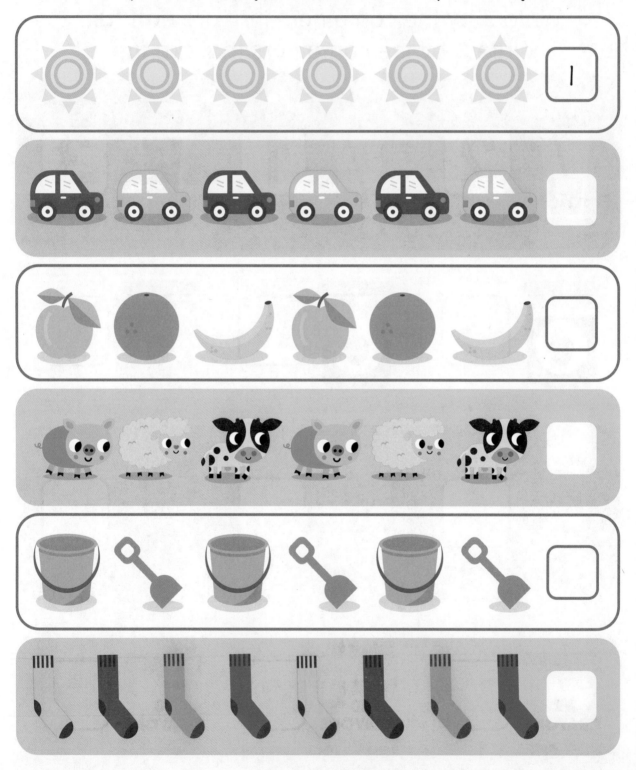

1

Pattern Hunt

Look for these **patterns** in your home.
Check the boxes as you find them.

☐ stripes

☐ polka dots

☐ checks

☐ zigzags

☐ diamonds

☐ waves

☐ flowers

☐ animal print

☐ plaid

Patterns We Wear

Match the **patterned** pajama tops
with their bottoms.

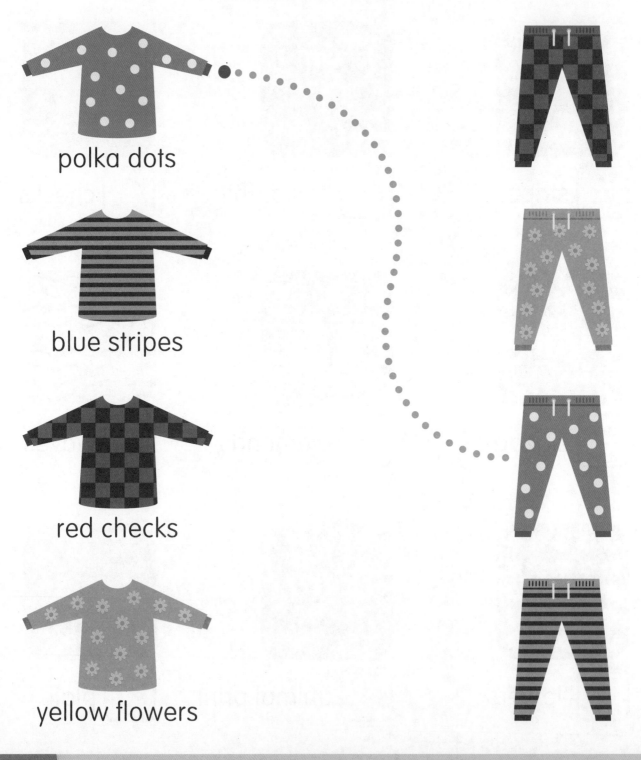

polka dots

blue stripes

red checks

yellow flowers

Patterns on Animals

Match the **patterns** to the animals.

zebra

turtle

leopard

snake

What Comes Next?

Circle the thing that comes next in each **pattern**.

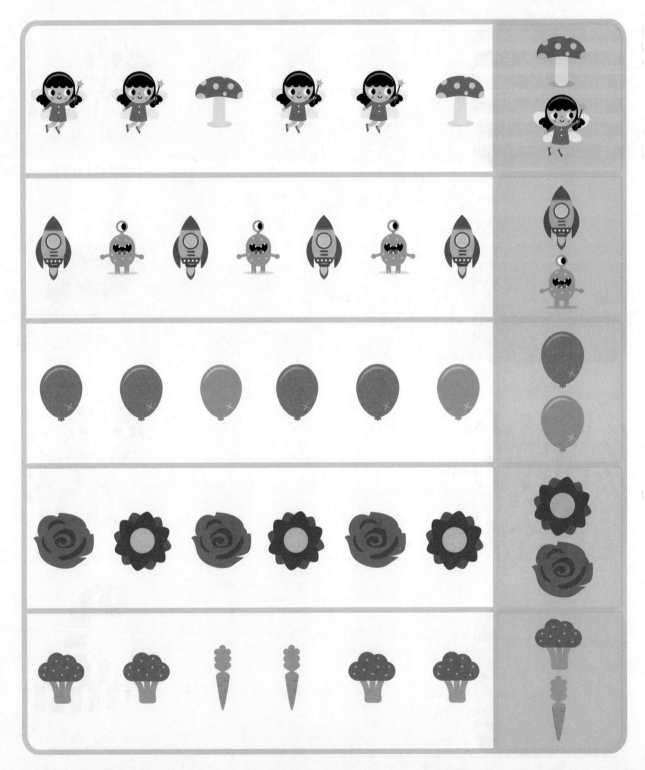

What Comes Next?

Draw what comes next in each **pattern**.

Draw your **own pattern** here.

Repeat the Pattern

Color the shapes to finish the **patterns**.

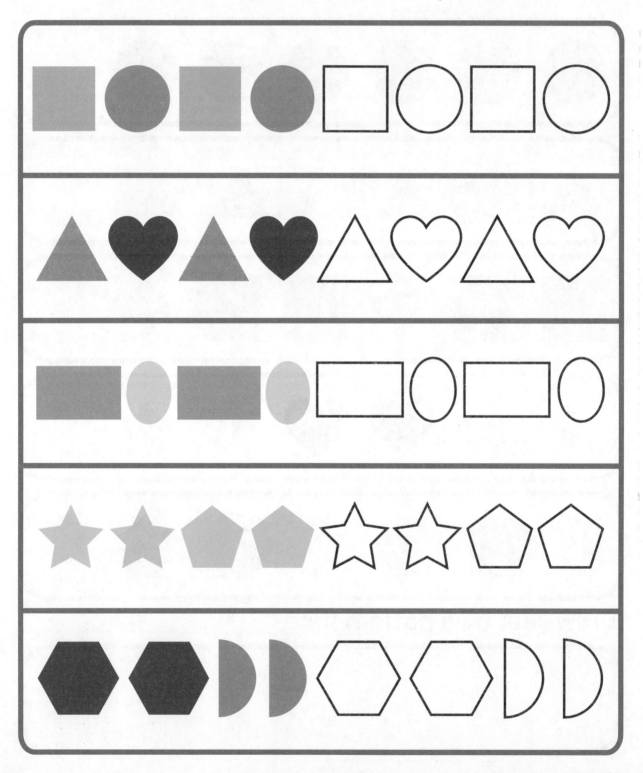

Block Patterns

Finish coloring the
block tower **patterns**.

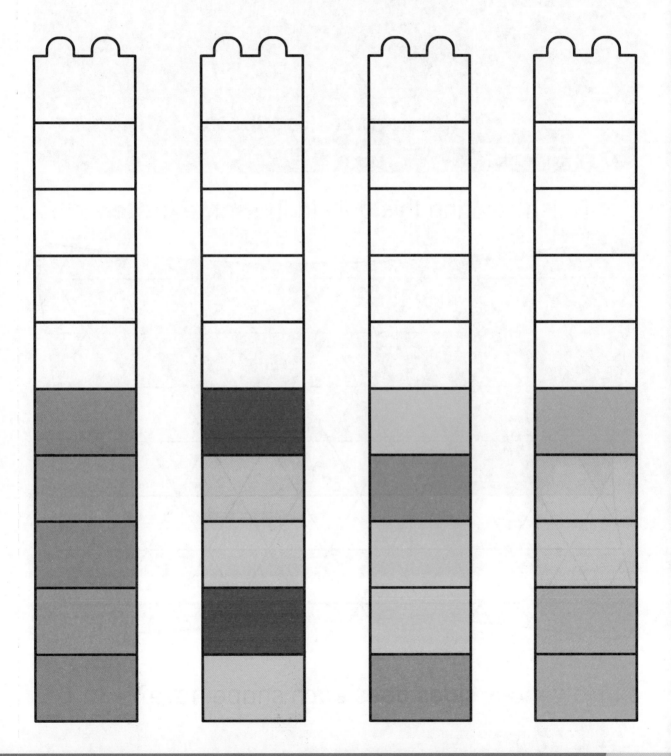

Patchwork Patterns

Circle the **shape** that makes up this patchwork quilt.

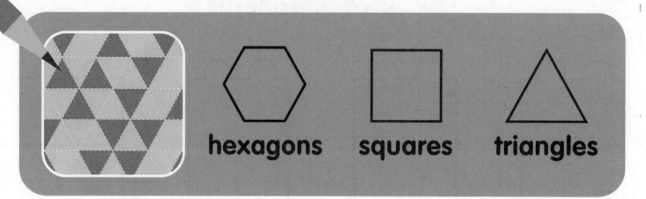

hexagons   squares   triangles

Finish coloring this quilt in the same **pattern**.

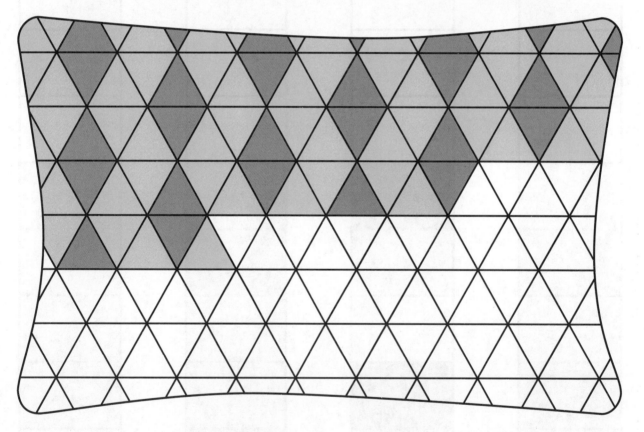

How many **sides** does each shape have?

Honeycomb Patterns

Circle the **shape** that makes up the honeycomb.

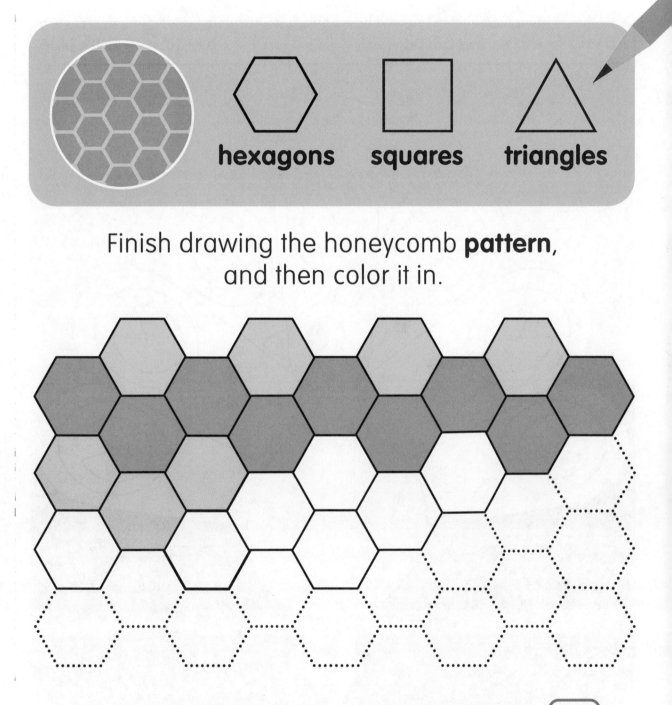

hexagons   squares   triangles

Finish drawing the honeycomb **pattern**,
and then color it in.

How many **sides** does each shape have?

Pattern by Numbers

Use the number key to color the **pattern**.

Key: 1 = green, 2 = purple, 3 = light blue, 4 = orange, 5 = dark blue

Pattern by Shapes

Use the shapes key to color the **pattern**.

Key: ⬡ = yellow, ⬜ = pink, ◇ = orange

Find the Differences

Circle the **3 differences** between the pictures.

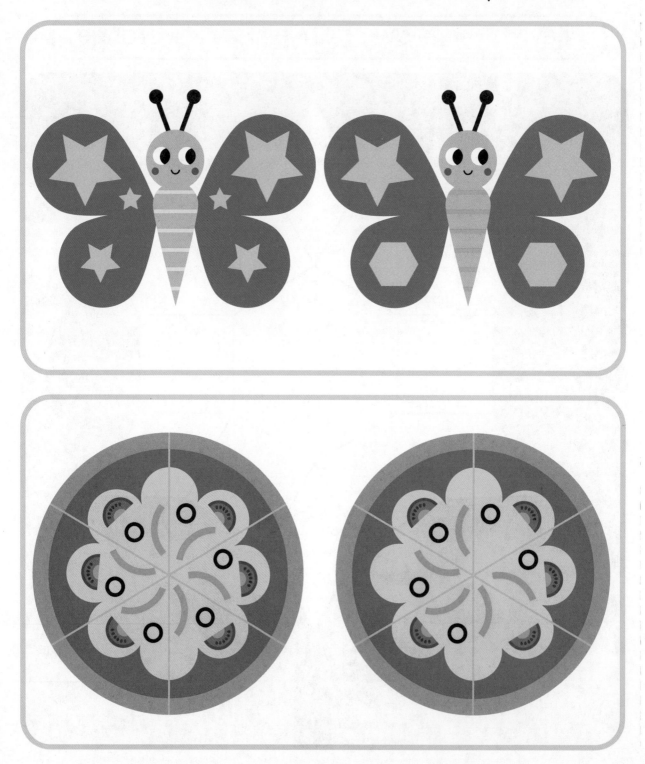

Order the Patterns

Number these pictures in the **order they happen**.

midday	nighttime	morning	evening
		1	

spring	winter	summer	fall
1			

caterpillar	butterfly	egg	cocoon
		1	

255

All About Animals

Draw lines to match the sentences about **animals** to the pictures.

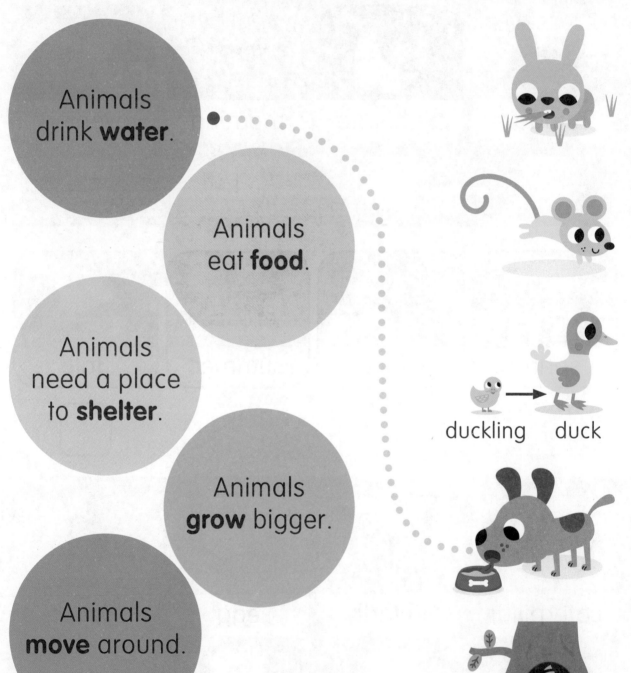

Animals drink **water**.

Animals eat **food**.

Animals need a place to **shelter**.

Animals **grow** bigger.

Animals **move** around.

duckling   duck

All About Plants

Draw lines to match the sentences about **plants** to the pictures.

Plants **grow** bigger.

Plants need **sunshine**.

Plants need **water**.

Plants have roots and **stay** in place.

Trees have a **wooden trunk** to hold them up.

trunk

roots

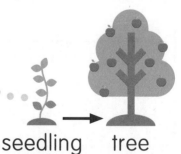
seedling   tree

Types of Plants

Write the correct **plant name** under each picture.

rose bush   grape vine   apple tree

pine tree   fern   palm tree

fern

Types of Animals

Write the correct **animal group** below each picture.
Use the **flowchart** to help you.

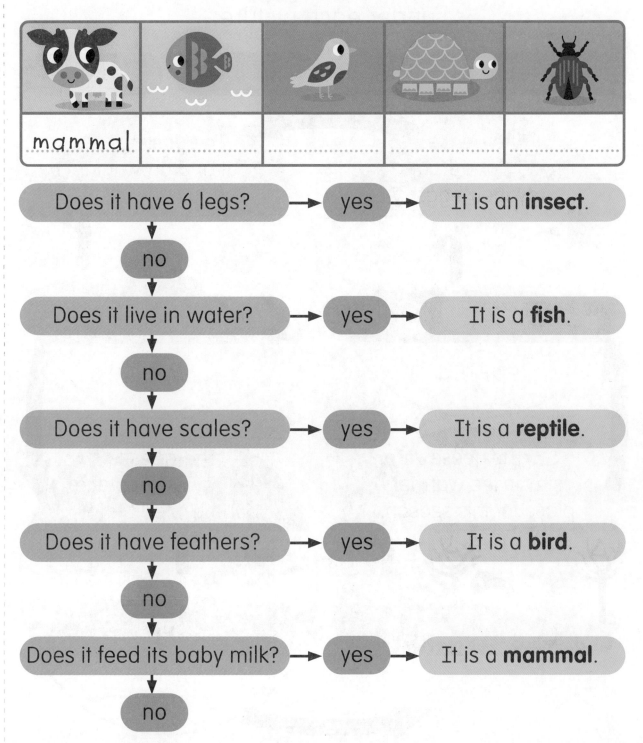

mammal				

Does it have 6 legs? → yes → It is an **insect**.

no

Does it live in water? → yes → It is a **fish**.

no

Does it have scales? → yes → It is a **reptile**.

no

Does it have feathers? → yes → It is a **bird**.

no

Does it feed its baby milk? → yes → It is a **mammal**.

no

A Year with Geese

Some geese fly to and from Canada and the United States every year. Write the correct **season** under each picture.

summer   winter   spring   fall

The geese fly to Canada and lay their eggs.

spring

The goslings eat and grow into adult geese.

....

The geese stay in the warmer place for this season.

....

The geese fly to a warm place in the United States.

....

Parts of a Tree

Write the correct word on each label to finish the **tree diagram**.

leaf   root   trunk   branch

Ancient Animals

These **reptiles** lived **long ago**. Use the words below to finish the sentences.

| water | wings | fins | land |

Pterosaurs could fly.

They had ....

Dinosaurs had legs.

They lived on ....

Ichthyosaurs swam

in ....

They had ....

The Human Body

Use the **body words** below to finish labeling the **diagram**.

hand　eye　leg　foot　mouth　knee

head

nose

ear

shoulder

arm

elbow

stomach

Land and Ocean

Circle the correct word to end each sentence.
Use the **map** to help you.

Kangaroos live in

| Australia | Antarctica |

There are lions in

| South America | Africa |

Madagascar is in the

| Indian Ocean | Atlantic Ocean |

New Zealand is in the

| Arctic Ocean | Pacific Ocean |

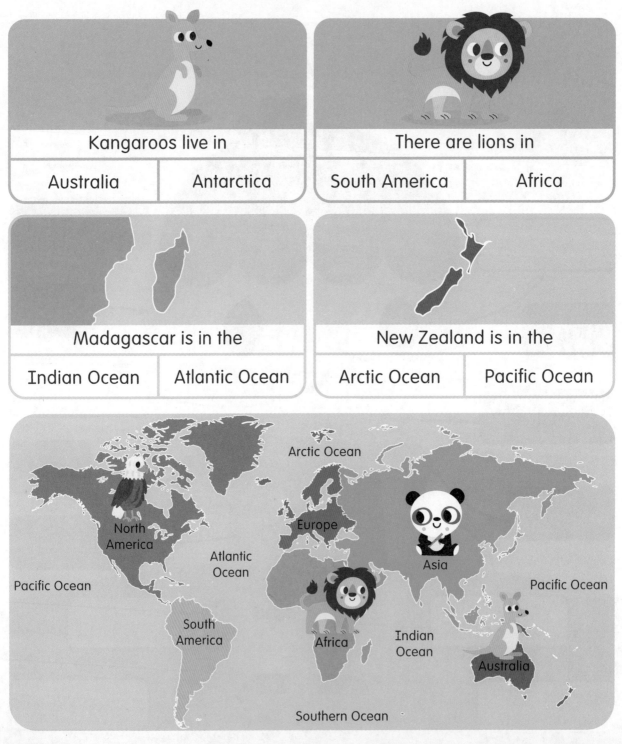

The Solar System

Color the **Sun** and the **8 planets** that move around it.
Use the color key.

Key: Earth = green & blue,   Jupiter = brown,
Mars = red,   Mercury = orange,   Neptune = pink,
Saturn = dark blue,   Sun = yellow,
Uranus = light blue,   Venus = purple

Using Energy

Plants get **energy** from the sun. Animals get **energy** from their food. In each row, circle the thing that uses the **energy source** on the left.

Energy Source	Living Things		
worm	tree	bird	person
grass	daisy	lion	cow
sun	fish	plant	zebra

Energy Source	Machines		
battery	TV	flashlight	scissors
gas	car	can opener	computer
electricity from a plug	watch	lamp	stapler

Marvelous Machines

Machines can give us heat, light, movement, and sound. Write **heat**, **light**, **move**, or **sound** under each machine.

Will It Stretch?

Some materials can **stretch** without breaking.
Put a **check** beside the things that are **stretchy**.
Put a **cross** by the things that **can't stretch**.

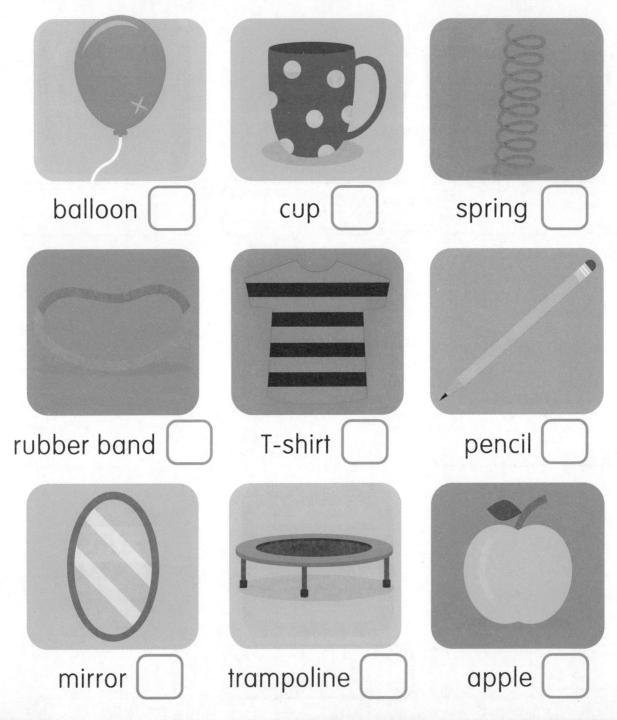

balloon ☐

cup ☐

spring ☐

rubber band ☐

T-shirt ☐

pencil ☐

mirror ☐

trampoline ☐

apple ☐

Is It See-Through?

Some materials are see-through, or **transparent**. Other materials are not see-through; they are **opaque**. Draw lines to match the objects with the words in the middle.

window

backpack

see-through

sweater

not see-through

ice cubes

glass

book

glasses

Fast or Slow?

Some things are **fast**, and some are **slow**.
Circle the one that would **win a race** in each pair.

baby
versus
child

rocket
versus
hot-air balloon

tortoise
versus
cheetah

bicycle
versus
motorcycle

Up or Down?

Draw lines to match the pictures with the words in the middle.

going up

going down

Push or Pull?

Circle the things being **pushed** with a **red** pencil.
Circle the things being **pulled** with a **blue** pencil.

Grip or Slide?

Rough surfaces help us **grip**. They have **lots of friction**. Smooth surfaces help us **slide**. They have **little friction**. Write **grip** or **slide** under each picture.

ice skates

hiking boots

slide

cleats

mountain bike tire

sled

Save Energy

Some things we do **save energy** and other things **waste energy**. Write **yes** or **no** after each question below.

Should you turn off the lights when you leave the room?

Should you open the windows when the heat is on?

Should you unplug devices when you are not using them?

If it is cold, should you put on a sweater instead of the heat?

Should you leave the fridge open while you choose what to eat?

If it is cold, should leave the front door open while you talk?

Save Resources

Some things we do **save resources** and other things **waste resources**. Write **yes** or **no** after each question below.

Should you turn off the faucet while you brush your teeth?

Should you fill the bathtub to the top every time?

Should you recycle plastic, paper, glass, and metal?

Should you use refillable bottles for your water?

Should you use only one side of a piece of paper?

Should you save leftovers for another meal?

Congratulations!

GREAT WORK AWARD

Name: ....

has successfully completed

GIANT KINDERGARTEN

Date: ....